The Pelican History of the United States

Volume 4

*

Unity and Culture

The United States,
1877-1900

H. Wayne Morgan

Allen Lane The Penguin Press

Advisory editor: Robert Divine

Copyright © H. Wayne Morgan, 1971

Allen Lane The Penguin Press
Vigo Street, London W1

ISBN 0 7139 0269 8

Printed in Great Britain by
Latimer Trend & Co. Ltd, Whitstable
Set in Monotype Baskerville

To Bob and Barbara Divine

Contents

Preface

THIS book is for the general reader rather than the academic historian. It introduces the post-Civil War generation that faced unprecedented challenges arising from rapid industrialization and entry into world affairs. The themes of developing national unity under the impact of these changes, and of the interchange of ideas between the United States and older cultures are explicit. But while interpreting events, I have tried to retain a sense of how they affected contemporaries. As Henry Seidel Canby has so judiciously remarked: 'The tendencies of a period, for a historian, may be more significant than the period, but that is not how those who lived them felt.'

The book contains four broad analytical essays rather than a chronological narrative. The treatment emphasizes the events, tastes, and values that affected most people alive at the time. Coverage is necessarily selective, and the Bibliographical Essay suggests further reading. This method hopefully will offer some insight into a fascinating era that produced a unified national spirit, and saw the United States enter world culture.

H. WAYNE MORGAN

The University of Texas
at Austin, Fall 1970

[1]

An Industrial Society

THE map of the United States in 1865 only outlined a great nation. Vast expanses of territory and a variety of natural resources awaited development. Differences of taste and custom illustrated the ages of the country's component sections. New England and parts of the South were settled in the early seventeenth century. The Old Northwest around the Great Lakes really dated from the late eighteenth century. The West Coast states were products of recent events. Boston, Chicago, New Orleans, and Seattle barely seemed in the same country. And the United States must now accommodate a flood of new population while seeking national cohesion.

'Americanism' was the necessary unifying doctrine for these restless populations and interests, but it had to be defined constantly in politics, economics, and social attitudes. The first generation to face a technological revolution that affected both national development and individual lives naturally reaffirmed the rhetoric that functioned in place of more formal unifying institutions such as monarchy or tradition. Individualism and expanding opportunity became common denominators for both settled Americans and immigrants. Their distaste for official planning that might inhibit personal freedom rested upon optimism about the future. In a country of such scope and variety, all things seemed possible. Cultural pluralism had merits, provided no authority controlled general goals or personal customs. These attitudes unified a people who steadfastly rejected formal ideology.

Industrialism existed before the war, but the conflict increased its momentum. The war also confirmed the central government's supremacy without enhancing its actual

power. It had no mandate beyond the emergency. To antici-
pate or organize the coming wave of industrialism was
beyond its purpose and capabilities. Both precedents for
regulation and expert information were lacking; these were
especially formidable obstacles in an economy of such
diversity and scope. The American people would not accept
state planning, and preferred to oversee economic growth
with regulations suited to specific grievances.

But despite talk of rugged individualism, laissez-faire
never governed. Politicians simply worked indirectly to
build a minimal general system that enlarged personal
opportunity. Government both promoted and regulated in
every major economic sector. Congress distributed cheap
land, and opened access to timber, water, and mineral resources. The army pacified the West and spent money in
under-developed areas. Congress was lenient about admit-
ting territories to the national system. Tariff protection,
internal improvements, and pension payments helped stabilize the 'home market'. Both federal and local agencies supported scientific research, agricultural experimentation,
and education.

The 'Industrial Revolution' was an abstraction, though
everyone saw its results in steam engines, railroads, wearing
apparel, processed foods, and advertising. In creating
markets, seeking efficiency, applying new technology, and
satisfying changing tastes, economic forces promoted
national unity.

Mere physical presence made the railroads symbolize
change. Rich with public domain but short of cash, the
federal government underwrote a transcontinental route
with land grants and bonds. The burden of construction and
future development passed to private hands, but the government received special rates to move troops, mail, and supplies, and held a mortgage. In 1899, the Central Pacific
settled all but 6 percent of its outstanding principal and
interest, and the Union Pacific cleared its obligation. Despite difficulties in raising capital, and fierce competition for

both present and future markets, by 1871 some 60,000 miles of track carried the country's goods. Activity was heaviest in the trunk system around the Great Lakes. Despite the depression of 1873–8, a total of 93,000 miles were in service by 1880. In 1890, 165,000 miles integrated the economy, and new construction began to level off. The rail system carried more debt, collected more revenue, and commanded more assets than the national government.

Railroad construction and organization was risky. Expensive western lines were built for future traffic. Despite public assistance, and significant foreign investment, capital was always scarce, and railroads were sensitive to economic fluctuations. But rapid cheap transportation was vital to the new economy. The rail network created national markets for both heavy industrial products and fragile household furnishings. Railroads both promoted and responded to urban demands for food, clothing, and building materials. And they helped develop areas producing raw materials, foodstuffs, and livestock.

Expansion was equally impressive in other sectors. Production of anthracite coal rose from 11 million tons in 1860 to 57 million in 1900. Crude petroleum increased from 500,000 barrels to 63,000,000 in the same period. Production of steel ingots, a basic index for heavy industrialization, rose from some 17,000 tons in 1867 to 7,000,000 in 1897. Three times as much wheat was grown in 1900 as in 1860, and exports went from 4,000,000 to 102,000,000 bushels. Cotton production nearly tripled. Growth rates in raw materials were almost as impressive, though staple agricultural prices declined in the face of world competition.

A shortage of skilled workers, and expanding markets, made large businesses adopt machinery and new technology. Scientific knowledge was especially important in improving textiles, steel, oil, railroad equipment, and consumer goods. Major concerns maintained laboratories, and experts culled scientific journals and reports of the world's learned societies for information and new techniques. With proverbial

yankee ingenuity, most businessmen were willing to learn
from anyone. 'While your metallurgists, as well as those of
France and Germany, have been devoting their time and
talents to the discovery of new processes', a Carnegie aide
told the British Iron and Steel Institute in 1881, 'we have
swallowed the information so generously tendered through
the printed reports of the Institute, and have selfishly
devoted ourselves to beating you in ouput.'[1]

Americans used Louis Pasteur's milk purification process
more readily than Frenchmen did. German and Swiss experts helped the new chemical industry improve such varied
products as textile dyes and drugs. Many new techniques
hastened economic expansion and diversification. 'American industry derived advantages from this period in which
the nation had to be economical, which it will never out-
live', the German psychologist Hugo Munsterberg noted in
1904.[2] Both workers and consumers accepted mechanization, though handicrafts still flourished, and sophisticated
machinery produced a remarkable array of attractive and
functional goods.

Observers over-rated the total impact of railroad construction on the economy, but builders spent vast sums for
wood, coal, steel, and equipment. After over-building in the
1870s, major lines increased expenditures for safety equipment, better cars, repair facilities, and improved roadbeds.
The telegraph system provided rapid communication, and
a revolution in printing created a new kind of advertising
business. And in 1898, the United States had 800,000 tele-
phone sets, twice as many as in all of Europe.

The enlarging markets, glamorous new enterprises, and
consumer goods were impressive, but uncertainty dogged
businessmen. Speculators threatened solid developers.
Labor became restless as production increased; and technological innovations cost money. And the inter-dependence
of a growing world system put the most cautious entre-
preneur at the mercy of forces he could not see, let alone
control. Business was good, but seldom safe.

The impressive statistics of increased production were national indexes, but the expanding economy naturally developed soft spots in both production and consumption. Industrialism inevitably did not spread benefits evenly, and agriculture paid a large share of industrialism's cost. Rapidly growing cities consumed dairy products, poultry and eggs, truck crops, and meat, which satisfied farmers with easy access to urban consumers. But cotton and wheat growers faced stiff world competition, bad weather, and a weak credit system. American history revealed many agrarian efforts to enact dislike of cities and business into law. While the political structure remained balanced, farmers had disproportionate strength in both parties.

Thousands of farmers bought new equipment, and luxuries like pianos and books for the parlor. Government agencies and the educational system developed better animal care, pest control, and processing techniques. But farm journals and spokesmen decried the flight of youth to city jobs. Urban life appealed to the young, no matter how often elders attacked the alleged decline of morality and American values in the cities.

Agriculture improved in specific sectors, and for countless individuals, but farming declined as a way of life. Weed-choked roads, fallen fences, and deserted houses testified to rural New England's decay. The young went to textile mills, or aspired to enter such sophisticated business as insurance in Hartford, or merchandising in New York. In the West, Hamlin Garland and other local colorists lamented the erosion of a unique regional culture in the face of national unity and world tastes.

The South was the most obvious absentee from industrialism's table of plenty. The ceremonial end of Reconstruction in 1877 did not spark either reunion or economic revival, and the area turned inward. Accurate statistics were hard to compile for an economy based on small farming, but Southern *per capita* wealth was barely half the national average. As the 1880s opened, parts of Charleston and Columbia were still blackened. In the countryside, ruined houses, fallen bridges, and archaic attitudes all showed how little had changed.

There was neither the governmental mechanism nor the public disposition to aid the area directly. In the 1880s, Henry W. Grady, Atlanta newspaper editor and orator, promoted the 'New South Idea', frankly hoping to attract private capital. Southerners should accept industrialism, which was better than any dead past. 'I see a South the home of fifty millions of people,' he trumpeted, 'her cities vast hives of industry; her countryside the treasures from which their resources are drawn; her streams vocal with whirring spindles.'[3]

Grady died young, but his idea made some progress. A few New England textile mills moved south; steel and coal came to Birmingham. Even agriculture diversified somewhat to grow more sugar, citrus, and rice. Production of raw materials such as lumber, turpentine, flax, and ores increased. Cities grew, but the urban-industrial spirit made little headway against ingrained conservatism, and did not even blur the edges of the race question. Good intentions, hard work, and official favoritism to industry could not quickly overcome poor educational facilities, a weak credit system, and hostility to outside influences. The southern economy improved, but lagged behind national growth. In 1905, Henry James noted that a romanticized past and fear of racial conflict isolated the section. 'I recognized something more than the melancholy of a lost cause. The whole infelicity speaks of a cause that could never have been gained.'[4] And was therefore binding in defeat, he might have added. The South was always less a victim of national power than of her stubborn resistance to change.

By the mid 1880s, the economy had acquired a disturbing self-direction. Men planned yet were never secure. A system that produced more and better goods obviously required unified manufacturing and distribution. The individualistic ethic that united Americans ironically seemed to create impersonal economic power. Because it served the whole economy, yet influenced individual lives, the railroad became the chief object of public concern about an impersonal corporate system. The criticism had its ironies. Most towns welcomed lines to raise property values, promote settlement, bring industry, and join new markets. But after passing bond issues or granting tax favors, the same communities often saw 'The Octopus' in all railroad tracks, and made every director a 'Robber Baron.'

Much of the rail system's bad press reflected emotion. Almost anyone could discover evil in profitable machinery under distant control that traversed former public domain. And railroad influence in politics, a prime target of reformers, was often baleful. The dislike of railroad power also symptomized tensions between city and countryside, East and West, rich and poor, as industrialism unified the national economy but seemed to threaten old ideals.

Diagnoses were easier to find than solutions that would satisfy the railroad's diverse constituency without inhibiting growth. Agrarians complained of discriminations, but were not united. Those serving urban consumers wanted ready access to markets, and resented low long-haul shipping rates that helped western growers dominate cereal and meat production. Many influential eastern and midwestern shippers also wanted stable rates. And wary railroad managers hoped to end over-building, stock manipulating, and rate wars. If regulations must come, many railroad men reasoned, let Congress devise general guidelines for interstate traffic. New safety procedures, equipment, and practical schedules would follow. In 1885, a leading business journal neatly summarized the confusion:

Thus the curious spectacle is presented of friend and opponent alike pleading for redress at the hands of the government. The mercantile community asks that violent fluctuations in rates be done away with, that drawbacks and rebates be made impossible, that no more be charged for a long haul than a short one, that discrimination be abolished, that diversion of freight be no longer

permitted, and that various other grievances, real or imaginary,
be attended to. The railroads, too, now look to the government to
help them out of their difficulties . . . . In a word, merchants want
to be protected against themselves, and investors against both.
And they all cry for the same soothing syrup – legislative enact-
ment.[5]

The most vociferous critics testified to a persistent faith in
law by demanding simple prohibition of pooling, free passes,
rebates, and rate variations. But others favored a regulatory
commission, to establish workable guidelines. Its mere
existence hopefully would inhibit malpractices, and promote out-of-court settlements beneficial to individual liti-
gants.

In 1887, Congress established the Interstate Commerce
Commission, with power to regulate inter-state shipping,
gather information, and require 'reasonable and just'
charges. Though it could not fix rates, the Commission
could institute suits. Fear of government control, hazy legal
precedents, and political necessity all produced the compromise. In the broadest sense, the Act recognized consolidation's tangential inequities. In contrast to other
industrializing nations, the United States was now more
concerned to regulate than to promote basic industries.

The ICC Act was a precedent for future regulation, but
did not end debate over the economy's direction or form.
The improved communications and advertising that helped
businessmen sell goods also ironically harmed their public
image. There had always been rich and poor men, but
wealth on the scale of John D. Rockefeller or William H.
Vanderbilt was now conspicuous. Small concerns still trans-
acted most of the nation's business, but many basic enterprises seemed concentrated in a few hands. The word
'trust' entered popular parlance, and critics argued that
business had forgotten its public constituency. In 1889,
the economist George Gunton snapped that 'the public
mind has begun to assume a state of apprehension, almost
amounting to alarm' concerning big business.[6]

An era and a people concerned with orderly growth naturally liked what most corporations produced. Nostalgic images of neighborhood tailors and corner grocers omitted high prices, poor stocks, and uncertain deliveries. But the efficiency registered in declining rates and faster service did not spare the railroads from hostility and regulation. Americans took pride in an innovative economy, but were bound to distrust an impersonal corporation and a new managerial class that seemed to violate the individualistic ethic. 'These men whom we disliked were of the new industrial type', Henry Seidel Canby recalled, 'hardened by competition and impersonal because their success came from selling the products of machines.'[7] The public had material grievances, but its indictment was moralistic at heart: big business was unfair to competitors, and had undue political influence. Yet the public would not destroy efficient or productive bigness; it merely wished to eliminate specific practices that threatened competition or social stability.

Criticism accompanied industrial expansion, but supporters of anti-trust regulation divided over aims and means. Some reformers wished to curb the role of business in American life; others saw material success as the key to stable democracy. Even labor spokesmen feared bureaucracy and anti-monopoly laws that might apply to unions. Workers might gain more from big business than from a welter of small units. 'We view the trusts from the standpoint that they are our employers', Samuel Gompers said, 'and the employer who is fair to us, whether an individual, or a collection of individuals . . . in the form of a corporation or a trust, matters little to us so long as we obtain fair conditions'.[8] Craft unions at least tended to accept corporations that recognized labor's right to organize.

Like all great public questions, the trust issue required a national political measure, both to attack the problem and to signify concern. In 1890, Senator John Sherman of Ohio authored a regulatory act that outlawed every 'contract, combination in the form of trust or otherwise, or conspiracy in restraint of trade or commerce. . .'. Though unions were not mentioned in the law, Sherman and other spokesmen exempted them from coverage. Lacking constitutional guidelines and precedent, the measure went as far as most people desired. 'All we, as lawmakers, can do is declare general principles', Sherman insisted. He also vigorously denied attacking business:

The bill does not seek to cripple combinations of capital and labor, the formation of partnerships or of corporations, but only to prevent and control combinations made with a view to prevent competition, or for the restraint of trade, or to increase the profits of the producers at the cost of the consumer. It is the unlawful combination, tested by the rules of common law and human experience, that is aimed at by this bill, and not the lawful and useful combination.[9]

The Sherman Act was unenforceable. Whatever its protestations, every administration tacitly accepted President Theodore Roosevelt's astute separation of bigness and badness. The 'good trust' that obeyed competitive rules and produced sound products would likely escape government censure. Businessmen who violated unwritten codes or explicit laws risked damaging publicity and legal penalty. As the next generation of reformers discovered, it was easier to suggest remedies than to achieve cures for economic imbalance when the world economy moved steadily toward standardization.

Laws defined specific boundaries that businessmen could not ignore, but legislation affected their daily activities less than pressures from labor and consumers. Despite confusion over aims and methods, unionization paralleled corporate growth. There was no 'working class' comparable to Europe's, but skilled laborers quickly perceived their critical role in basic industries. The union movement lacked central direction, but spokesmen easily used the public's suspicion of corporate power. Except during violent strikes, most Americans approved labor's effort to gain material advantage and bargaining status.

Many businessmen, especially of an older generation, were naturally hostile. Collective bargaining was an effort to get something for nothing; unions would profit from the businessman's risks. The old sense of identity between employer and worker eroded rapidly under the pressures of mechanization and expansion. Corporate directors and planners lost contact with producers. And small owners thought 'the men' were 'collectively troublesome, but as individuals liked and trusted'.[10]

Despite confused economic change, the worker's general condition improved. Real wages increased because of declining prices, reflecting the paradox of continuous expansion and competition despite recessions. Critically placed special unions won considerable gains. Few employers wished to antagonize workers and risk losing their skills or loyalty, and often spread work in hard times. Some businessmen perceived the basic truth that wages came back in purchases. 'You cannot have low and depressed labor and a prosperous business or a prosperous country', one told a Senate committee.[11] For every flinty opponent of labor, there was a Mark Hanna who thought only fools refused to meet their men half-way.

In the 1880s, the Knights of Labor seemed on the verge of organizing a national union to promote both social action and material self-interest. But internal quarrels, conflicting interests among workers, and public condemnation of the violence that often accompanied strikes broke up the Knights. Smaller units, seeking immediate goals, suited both the workers' taste and economic realities. The American Federation of Labor, and the railway brotherhoods that organized specific skilled workers, typified the craft unionism that responded to economic change. In 1897, some 250,000 men paid A. F. of L. dues; in 1904, about 1,700,000, and only 7 percent of the national work force was unionized. Labor never built a united front, or adopted large European-style goals.

Business opposition alone did not explain labor's in-

ability, if not refusal, to seek more than rising wages and
better working conditions. While recognizing the need of
bargaining power, many workers identified unions with
lay-offs and violence. Labor was also as diversified as industry and lacked the funds or compatible aims necessary for
unity. Organizers competed with each other, and quarrelled
over methods. Most workers suspected corporate power, but
wished to eliminate specific inequities and gain security.

The reformist dream of consolidating all marginal groups
into one crusade ignored their contradictory prejudices and
desires. Workers often shared more attitudes with the
successful men they hoped to emulate than with social
critics. Where mutual trust and cooperation prevailed,
employers and employees believed they grappled with 'the
real world'. Pride of accomplishment accorded status, and
smoothed over many tensions. Workers also saw men as
individuals, not abstract masses, and doubted the reformist
doctrines of human perfectibility and rational planning.

Several violent upheavals marked organized labor's
halting progress. In 1877, a strike disrupted eastern rail
traffic, and President Hayes answered local appeals for
federal troops to end disorder. The Homestead steel strike of
1892 had national repercussions. And in 1894, the Pullman
strike wracked Chicago with violence that ended with the
arrival of token federal forces.

Some observers saw anarchy or socialism in such dis-
turbances, and talked darkly of warfare between the Haves
and Have-nots. But disorders usually reflected hard times
or local situations rather than a desire to destroy the system.
Socialism appealed more to thinkers than to doers. A
formal socialistic system repelled most Americans, who
feared it would level downward in seeking equality. Workers
disdained the term 'working class', and assumed they could
move within an expanding system. Though few laborers rose
to command corporations, men did rise in politics, the other
great avenue of worldly success. And to those involved,
movements from semi-skilled to skilled jobs, or from

apprentice to foreman, were as significant as a change from over-alls to white shirts. As a visiting Englishman noted: 'Every American carries a marshal's baton in his knapsack in a way that has hardly ever been true in Europe'.[12]

Unions became the workers' instrument precisely because they avoided ideology and offered a sense of community and power that tempered corporate impersonality. They also combined individualism and group action. These responses produced a conservative movement, dedicated to the piece-meal advancement of general interests. Unions were not the vanguard of a general reform urge, but their pragmatism reflected the workers' belief in the new industrial society's opportunities.[13]

Yet no one denied business opposition to unionization, and the worker's share of real gain lagged behind the investor's. Conditions and wages depended on particular jobs, and the labor market. Neither business nor unions sought to help the Negro, Chinese, or unskilled immigrants except by expanding the economy. These lapses were part of the same individualistic ethic that shaped the workers' optimistic pragmatism. Times were sometimes hard, but the era as a whole seemed prosperous and expansive. By 1900, many workers doubtless agreed with Gompers's tart response to the suggestion that remorseless capital was impoverishing the masses: 'Oh, that is perfectly absurd'.[14]

The absorption of immigrants was a striking as economic growth. In the 1870s, some 2,600,000 people entered the country; another 5,000,000 followed in the 1880s. About 4,000,000 made the ocean voyage in the uncertain 1890s. The country needed population, but the sudden influx of diverse talents and customs inevitably produced friction. Opposition to Chinese immigration was a major issue in the West, and touched national politics in the presidential campaigns of 1876 and 1880. Unions hoped to keep skilled labor in short supply, and secured legislation to regulate overseas recruitment. Organizers naturally feared cheap labor that might depress wages or break strikes. 'Immigrants work for almost nothing and seem to be able to live on wind', a Wisconsin worker complained, 'something which I cannot do'. Another believed that immigration 'brings wages down below the breadline'.[15] But except for minor specific exclusions, the government maintained virtually an open-door policy.

Many German and Scandinavian families settled in the plains states and Old Northwest. They also brought the arts of brewing to Milwaukee and St. Louis, and worked as craftsmen in Chicago and Minneapolis. The Irish settled first in port cities. Later immigrants created enclaves in every major city of citizens from the Baltic and Mediter-ranean lands, Central Europe, and the Balkans.

Settled Americans admired the virtues of thrift, hard work, and enterprise which the Germans allegedly typified. But the drunken Irishman and incoherent Italian were stock humor characters, objects of some doubt about civiliza-tion's progress. Yet it was a common saying that Irish picks and shovels built America's streets, while Italian shoulders bore the hods of bricks and mortar for her new buildings.

But despite uncertain language and strange tastes, most immigrants had some skill. Even desperate men did not leave family and homeland without the ability to earn a living in a strange new world. Cornish miners helped to develop coal fields, and practiced tin- and copper-smithing. Central Europeans worked as masons, cabinet-makers, and glaziers. Still other immigrants were craftsmen in the decor-ative arts, furniture design and manufacture, and printing. A few had critical expertise in chemistry, geology, metal-lurgy, mathematics, and medicine. All in turn became consumers and contributed immensely to economic growth and to America's diverse culture.

Eager to succeed and gain recognition, most newcomers embraced americanization, provided it did not threaten personal customs or the right to support Old World nationalities. The government made no effort to settle immi-grants in particular sections, and citizenship was easy to obtain. 'Other lands grant only asylum', Henry Sienkiewiecz noted in the 1870s, 'this land recognizes the immigrant as a son and grants him rights.'[16]

The first generation's lot was usually hard, and the unskilled paid a large share of industrialism's cost. Yet most immigrants were hopeful and infinitely better off than in Europe, and quickly developed social and religious organizations that gave 'Little Italy' or 'Little Poland' a sense of belonging to America without the loss of past attachments. The typical newcomer believed his children would move beyond his present role. He appreciated the traditional American emphasis on work as evidence of merit, generalized education, and distaste for social classes. Henry James distrusted foreigners, but saw the force behind the immigrant's energy: 'Whatever he might see himself becoming, he was never to see himself that again, any more than you were ever to see him'.[17]

Growing cities were industrialism's chief monuments. Horatio Alger's success reflected the confrontation of rural attitudes and urban tastes and beliefs. But there was more to the city's appeal than surface glamor. In 1899, Adna Ferrin Weber, the greatest contemporary student of urbanization, noted the attractions of city life:

The village is dull not only to the man pursuing light amusements, but to him who seeks cultivated associations, for in these days the cities are the centers of intellect as of wealth. Even the college town with its intellectual atmosphere is to many highminded people less stimulating than the city, where intellectual ability is much more varied.[18]

The rate and quantity of urban growth were impressive. In 1860, only 141 places had populations over 8000; the number had risen to 545 by 1900. Within the same time span, city population increased from 5,000,000 to 25,000,000. In 1890, most urbanites resided in the Northeast, and New York remained the chief national city; but the rate of growth was more spectacular elsewhere. Chicago's expansion seemed endless as it dominated rail traffic and Great

Lakes shipping and processed much of the world's food. The percentage of urban dwellers was highest in the sparsely settled West. Denver's population increased from 4700 in 1870 to 110,000 in 1890, as the city serviced Rocky Mountain mining and livestock enterprises. The pre-war urban pattern filled out, but cities grew at critical points to meet new economic needs. Duluth processed wheat from the northern plains and Birmingham accommodated a new steel industry.

Cities provided jobs for both the unskilled and artisans, expanded old enterprises and supported new ones. Bricks and marble, wood and foodstuffs came from the countryside. Construction absorbed huge quantities of cement and steel, special pipe for water and sewerage, and fixtures for gas and electricity. The statistics of city expansion were as impressive as those for railroad building or wheat production. Municipal indebtedness went from $200,000,000 in 1860 to $725,000,000 in 1880, and $1,400,000,000 in 1902. Municipal waterworks were valued at $1,000,000,000 in 1900. Electric power stations did not exist in 1860, but by 1902 this glamorous new industry had issued $600,000,000 in stock. At the same time, private city transportation systems were funded at nearly $2,500,000,000. Though borrowing financed most capital outlays, local taxation took about 6 percent of the national income, twice the federal government's share.

Services inevitably lagged behind needs. Rural dominated legislatures restrained the city governments they chartered. Industry often operated beyond city limits to escape taxation, and the development of suburbs narrowed the inner city's tax base. The tendency toward central mass inflated real estate valuations, but increased the demands for expensive services. One new skyscraper required more water, heat, and power than a whole block of older buildings. Housing was scarce, and dirt roads skirted the edges of New York and Boston. And the horses that pulled fancy rigs, milk wagons, delivery drays, and streetcars posed special sanitation problems. They created street-sweeping jobs for an alderman's unskilled constituents, but imparted a special odor to nearly every section of a city.

Builders soon mastered the complex requirements of the new structures that served industrialism, but architecture revealed the era's hesitations and search for distinctive taste. American architecture was always diverse; no one style fitted the country's varied climates, ages, or peoples. This lack of a central esthetic, and of official direction, allowed post-war architects to experiment both with revived styles and individual ideas. And while most clients readily accepted technical innovations, 'artistic' decoration had to cover internal functionalism to help avoid the appearance of mere materialism.

Client taste and building codes hampered architects, but some master designers appeared. The numerous homes for the wealthy which Richard Morris Hunt derived from French châteaux retained grace and individuality. Henry Hobson Richardson provided dignity and power in modified romanesque buildings. Boston's Trinity Church was not entirely successful, but revealed his ability to integrate impressive masses of rough stone with color and decorations. Richardson worked most successfully with suburban railway stations, public libraries, and private residences that blended into a natural setting. The popular firm of McKim, Mead and White insisted on integrating a building with its environment, and created many structures whose modified classical lines were both elegant and 'modern'. Though derived from French models, their Boston Public Library was graceful and functional.

Louis Sullivan followed the lead of John Wellborn Root, Daniel Burnham, and Denkmar Adler to become a famous member of the 'Chicago School'. Moving toward the doctrine that form followed function, Sullivan held that the skyscraper should not be muted or disguised. Upward motion expressed its purpose; proper design harmonized its mass. In emphasizing light, clean lines, and unifying decoration, Sullivan was distinctly 'modern', but did not break with the past. His designs contained many echoes of preceding styles, and his decorations recalled rural life.

New construction technology interested the average observer as much as external design, and there were innovations enough to fill many Sunday supplements. In cold climates, builders mixed salt with mortar and insulated fresh concrete with straw to prevent freezing. Specially manufactured steel beams and concrete reinforced with wire mesh increased structural safety. Skyscraper construction produced numerous time-saving methods and new comforts. Hot and cold water, gas, and insulated wires filled new flexible piping that adjusted to settling. Elevators and communication systems increased both comfort and efficiency. But innovation had limits, and clients were seldom willing to experiment with daring external designs. 'Modern commercial architecture in general . . . bears the scars of a conflict if not between the architect and the client, between the claims of utility and of art . . .' the critic Montgomery Schuyler noted.[19]

Like other arts, architecture retained a moral purpose in the public mind. Amid hurry, mass, and indifference, buildings should 'convey in some large elemental sense an idea of the great, stable, conserving forces of modern civilization', John Wellborn Root insisted.[20] And in arguing that form must accommodate function, Sullivan meant that a building should represent a total cultural purpose.

But the problem of combining industrial power and historic dignity baffled most designers. A modified *beaux-arts* style derived chiefly from France seemed to answer the need for individuality within a historical tradition. Most architects drew on *beaux-arts* training, which reinforced the international style's appeal, and they wanted buildings to create a sense of grandeur and continuity. Public places should 'foster unanimity of purpose where the common interest is set above private or individual interests'.[21] Romantic self-expression ignored society and tradition. Suitably modified Greek and Roman capitol buildings symbolized the historic continuity of legislative, judicial, and executive functions. The university and art museum should express a timeless purpose, not an era. And classical forms still could serve an industrial society. The railway station modelled on a Roman bath gave the traveler a sense of starting a significant journey and of arriving at an important place. Like all academicisms, the *beaux-arts* style became self-conscious and effete, but produced some remarkable works, and offered unity until people accepted industrial forms and functions.

The characteristic American distrust of bureaucratic planning for private property did not extend to public facilities. Frederick Law Olmstead's plan for Central Park typified efforts to save greenery from remorseless development. Whatever the merits of its neo-classical style, the Columbian Exposition of 1893 sparked widespread interest in parks, street planning, and monumental squares. Most cities retained some open space, suitably ornamented with statuary, plazas, and even zoos.

Most city dwellers rented apartments. Standardized tenements housed the poor, and various styles of row-housing accommodated middle income groups. Wealthier residents lived behind elegant brownstone fronts in planned enclaves. Every city had show sections for the rich, such as Gramercy Park in New York or Nob Hill in San Francisco. But the family home was a goal for nearly every wage-earner. A house and lot represented security and success. The new suburban home that figured in William Dean Howells' *The Rise of Silas Lapham* (1885) was a common compromise between rural isolation and urban tension for the expanding middle class.

House exteriors illustrated national diversity and varied tastes. On occasion they seemed to prove the adage that 'American humor has never found full expression except in architecture'.[22] Native 'Pennsylvania Dutch' or generic 'colonial' forms never disappeared, but an eclectic 'Queen

Anne' became the reigning formula. This endlessly modified style employed gables, dormer windows, and porches that invited decoration according to the occupant's success or pretensions. The most filigreed such houses were 'cases of disorderly conduct done in brick-work and stone'.[23] But they were often charming and distinctive, bearing the individual stamps of both artisans and owners.

Self-taught decorators and whipsaw salesmen did not discourage this straining toward ornamentation. But the good home interiors revealed American pragmatism at its best. Floor plans often separated rooms according to use, and wide halls eased the passage of children and adults. Bays added light and view to rooms, while tall windows and high ceilings created both spaciousness and harmony. The porch and 'stoop' became important institutions of social intercourse in both city and country.

American women quickly took advantage of technological innovations and cheap mass-produced household implements. Kitchens were rationalized, partly with examples from ship galleys and mass facilities such as barracks and hospitals. Hand operated sweepers and washing machines, steam irons, and carefully designed multi-purpose stoves reduced the housewife's drudgery and helped satisfy a general American desire for speed and comfort.[24] The use of paint and wallpaper to define rooms contrasted sharply with European treatment. A German visitor noted approvingly that '. . . the modern American house is built entirely from the inside out.'[25] Feminists urged housewives to emphasize family life and recreation. 'Home is peculiarly a place of rest', one decorator insisted, 'though the birthplace of all industries.'

Office furniture illustrated a penchant for comfort and mobility. Typewriter and swivel chairs, and desks, were often portable, and suited to their tasks. But they were not 'respectable', and entered the home only indirectly as the adjustable lounger, porch swing or hammock, and an astonishing array of collapsible camping equipment.

Formal 'parlor' furniture must have historical associations. It was not designed for lounging, but to remind guests and hosts of how far each had come or must go. Advances in machine finishing and design, and cheap transportation permitted the new furnishings industry to satisfy mass taste. Manufacturers boasted of putting a log in one end of a machine and extracting a bedroom suite from the other. 'Grand Rapids' styles based on mediterranean and baroque models prevailed in the 1870s, but Empire, Japanese, and regional American models were influential. Ornate pieces were popular because they had character and hand-made qualities; consumers still suspected some machine goods. The simple and utilitarian was too lacking in esthetic values for allegedly materialistic Americans.

Eclecticism permitted individual variations in the face of standardized groupings. Designers understood that time restored former tastes in world cycles, and no single style in anything suited American diversity. And furniture was often sensible beneath the decoration. The pigeon-hole desk was eminently functional; so was the bureau or sideboard with separate drawers. Deep tufting on sofas and chairs was ornamental, but also circulated air around the sitter. Velvet coverings produced either sheen or a rough texture. The tassels that fringed a 'turkish' sofa were decorative, but also diverted a child's toy. The light, inexpensive rattan and wicker furniture popular in warm climates could easily be changed with an inexpensive coat of paint.

A public thirsty for culture bought a great array of decorative items. Louis C. Tiffany turned from painting to design glass and pottery. His lampshades, tableware, vases, stained windows, jewelry, and *objets* emphasized color and elegance.[27] The Tiffany firm was 'decorator to the carriage trade', but also made inexpensive items for a larger public that liked 'modern' styling.

In a more traditional but equally rewarding manner, John Rogers, 'the People's Sculptor', tinged realism with familiarity. In the thirty years after 1860, his workshops sold

some 80,000 copies of plaster sculpture priced at about
$15.00. The best pieces were familiar symbolic scenes like
'Coming to the Parson', and 'The Chess Players'. A staunch
Unionist, Rogers pointed patriotic lessons with 'The Slave
Auction' of 1863, figures of common soldiers, and a famous
group of General Grant and Secretary Stanton advising
Lincoln.[28]

A flood of intricate toys acquainted children with prosaic
but important aspects of social change. Boys prized mechanical fire trucks and building assembly kits. Girls learned of
deportment and fashion from dolls and complex doll houses.
Both sexes fed ingenious mechanical banks, whose figures
performed elaborate feats to digest a penny or nickel.[29] The
same industry supplied colorful decorations for fraternal,
political, and religious groups; barbershops and circuses;
police and fire units. The cigar-store Indian and merry-go-
round horse were among its lasting artifacts.

American design was at its functional best in machinery
and tools. The famous Corliss Engine at the Centennial
Exposition of 1876 weighed nearly 1,700,000 pounds, ran a
great deal of machinery without noise or vibration, and displayed its working parts. The growing doctrine that function produced form was evident in clean designs for steam-
ships, locomotives, farm equipment, and horse-drawn
equipage. A German visitor to the Columbian Exposition
of 1893 appreciated displays of simple but stylish objects and
equipment.[30] But eager to lead the world on its stated terms,
Americans accepted foreign definitions of 'culture', and
found it hard to see 'culture' in locomotives or swivel chairs.
Culture involved contemplative and symbolic values tied to
the past; art must avoid the appearance of work or money.
This feeling of inferiority and sensitivity to charges of
materialism explained most of the division between decoration and utility.

With space to fill, resources to use, and the apparent chance
to gain security, Americans logically enthroned production.
Rejection of the idea of a permanent poor class made mass-

consumption and advertising more logical to Americans than to Europeans. Few comprehended economic nationalization, but nearly everyone felt its effects in the new food, clothing, leisure, and information that technology produced.

Meat became a staple of the American diet while still a luxury elsewhere because of efficient mechanized processes. Packers boasted of using everything in a pig except the squeal, and turned livestock into dressed carcasses and semi-finished cuts with a rapidity and cheapness no corner grocer could match. By the 1880s, Philip Armour's company shipped beef in iced-cars and expanded the housewife's choice of fresh meats in major cities. The same efficiency affected bread, another mass staple. Production and distribution were so uniform by 1916, that a raisin firm increased its sales ten-fold in two years by suggesting raisin-bread as a breakfast treat.

The lowly saltine illustrated the productive system's subtle effects on personal life. Wiseacres who fished in a country store's dirty cracker barrel said packaged crackers would go stale or break in transit. But the laboratory technicians were right. Careful packaging and good rail service kept them wholesome. Critics then said prosperous consumers would disdain crackers. But the advertising men were right. Crisp, clean saltines became a delicacy for matrons and a staple for children. Thus did technology confound folk wisdom.[31]

New department stores offered rapid service, competitive prices, and a large array of goods. Newspaper ads and mail order catalogues altered tastes in furnishings and equipment for both farm and home. The total process often hurt the small-town artisan. Harness-menders and blacksmiths gave way first to mail order goods and then to the automobile. Some declining trades adapted to competition. Many livery stable owners took up bicycle repair. The corner grocer and neighborhood tailor seemed threatened, yet mass distribution and consumption also helped the small merchant by increasing his stock.

The printed word was the chief agent of changing tastes and attitudes. The American lust for newspaper reportage was deeply ingrained, but technology vastly increased both available information and analysis. By the early 1880s, wire services offered world news to subscribers, and Henry Sienkiewicz thought that New York's dailies 'describe European events ahead of and more accurately than European newspapers'. Special correspondents discussed major events. The interested reader could follow every step of a presidential nominating convention's procedures in a morning edition, and read astute analysis and interviews with protagonists in the evening number. Advertising revenue reduced production costs, and standardized operations did not eliminate forthright editors such as Charles Dana of the New York *Sun*, or Joseph Medill of the Chicago *Tribune*. Small town publishers often retained national political influence, while catering to local interests. Newspaper reading was a form of public education, and Henry Sienkiewicz again saw its merit: 'American journalism accurately reflects the requirements of the American people, who read their newspapers for specific information relating to their political, industrial, and commercial affairs, and not for stylistic gems, wit, or literary flourishes'.[32]

Weekly and monthly journals furnished deeper coverage. *Harper's Weekly*, *Atlantic Monthly*, *North American Review*, and the *Nation* were only a few of the reviews analyzing world events, economics, or science. Improved steamship service brought European publications to artists, businessmen, and government officials within a week of issue. Special magazines dealt with religion, fashion, and education. Nearly every profession had an organ to disseminate information and develop its sense of community.

A technological revolution lay behind the printer's ability to satisfy new demands. Standard paper sizes, steam presses, and linotype machines speeded production. Improved binding processes, line drawing, and finally photography enriched book publishing, while an expanding readership and the growth of public libraries helped keep down retail prices.

Advertising appeals covered billboards and horsecar ceilings. Travelers read about the virtues of Bull Durham tobacco on the barns and fences of many a shrewd farmer who exchanged the space for a new paint job. Most of the advertising industry used the printed word, and by 1900, color posters and magazine pages tempted customers. Printed advertising outlays increased some 80 percent in the 1880s, and another one-third in the following decade. 'The man who has anything to sell now-a-days has attached to his establishment not only his salesmen, but his poet,' a magazine commented as early as 1869.[33]

Stories about the 'drummer', or traveling salesman, with slick city ways and a kit of fascinating samples, entered the vernacular. The new salesmanship kept pace with a flood of consumer goods, and local merchants adopted national brands to compete with mail order houses. But while production and distribution became national, pricing often remained local, since merchants competed in most areas.

The office bards who sang the praises of button shoes and Peruna tonic also promoted new styles of leisure. The bicycle embodied a national concern for speed and competition. The dangerous high model gave way to the chain-driven 'safety' with equal wheels in 1889. Cycling became a craze, complete with cross-country races and national conventions. Despite laments about declining morals and rising skirts, the young sought emancipating distance from watchful elders. The National League of American Wheelmen lobbied for better roads, street-lighting, and curbing.[34]

Nationalization subtly affected sports; local teams competed fiercely but wore similar uniforms and theoretically obeyed standard rules.[35] Baseball and football flourished on college campuses, though administrators often disapproved. 'I will not permit thirty men to travel four hundred miles merely to agitate a bag of wind', President A. D. White of Cornell wired President James B. Angell of Michigan in opposing a football match.[36] But realism soon triumphed, and organized athletics became a major outlet for student frustrations and boredom, lessening the violence that characterized collegiate life in small towns. Students who resented faculty indifference and local criticism also found unity and identity in sporting events. Few spectators or participants reflected on any game's symbolism, but baseball and football suited American energy and ideals. Careful rules insured competition; team cooperation did not eliminate individual stars; and the whole performance promoted self-reliance.

The schools and colleges that supported athletics were tangible evidence of a general commitment to education. In 1897–8, elementary schools enrolled over 15,000,000 pupils; secondary schools accommodated 600,000. Colleges and professional institutions trained about 200,000 students. Between 1870 and 1900, the college population rose from 1·6 percent of the 18–21 age group, to 4 percent, while the number of campuses increased from 563 to 977.

Length of compulsory schooling, resources, and teaching methods varied widely. The short term and one-room school were common in rural areas, where pupils had to harvest and plant. Instruction was most modern in urban districts, and like other enterprises, schools incorporated new ideas. The Germanic kindergarten, Swedish gymnastics, English manual arts, and Continental learning theories entered the curricula. The educational system was diffuse, but served national needs and reflected American character. Even the smallest school, that necessarily emphasized only the three R's, enlarged pupils' lives with geography, history, and literature.

Despite the growing belief that everyone was entitled to public education, few students progressed beyond high school. Many institutions compensated for this with extension work, manual training, and night classes for both aspiring adults and working youngsters. But vocational schooling implied a hierarchy that might penalize those with only manual skills. Some employers wanted workers trained at public expense, while unions feared a glutted labor market. Degrees were rungs on the social ladder, but spokesmen insisted that education had larger purposes. 'The end and aim of life is not simply to equip professional men', one commentator noted, 'it is not simply to equip people with the power to "do business"; it is not *simply* to enable people to earn a living.'[37]

Just how to combine 'practical' agricultural and mechanical studies with 'elevating' humanities and arts produced sharp debate among educators and public officials. The generation in charge of policy had matured in the Jacksonian era, which suspected the aristocratic tendencies of classical studies. Their customary insistence on establishing new universities or expanding older ones in small towns illustrated both distrust of urban values, and the rural ideal's tenacity.

Change seemed easier to attain in higher education than at the local level. The pre-war college system obviously could not satisfy the new industrial society's needs. Most institutions offered only a smattering of ancient languages and literature, moral philosophy, and the natural sciences. Resources were meager, and the Darwinian revolution had bypassed overworked and underpaid faculties. Andrew D. White of Cornell thought the average antebellum college was 'as stagnant as a Spanish convent, and as self-satisfied as a Bourbon duchy.'[38]

Amid debate over function, and tension between urban and rural interests, major state universities like those in California, Michigan, Illinois, and Wisconsin diversified. The establishment and funding of private universities dedicated to post-graduate specialization such as Cornell (1853), Johns Hopkins (1876), Chicago (1890), and Stanford (1891), rivalled empire-building and innovation in steel or rails. Reform came to Harvard, but Princeton and Yale remained traditional. A few endowments reflected the country's growth. Johns Hopkins received $3,500,000 from its founder. Leland Stanford left assets valued at $24,000,000 to the institution that honored his son's memory. John D. Rockefeller gave $34,000,000 over many years to the University of Chicago.

As with corporate assets, the figures were often more impressive than assuring. Most private universities were financially insecure, and public institutions relied on state aid. Most funds went for buildings and equipment, and the temptation to over-expand was hard to resist. Like corporations, universities competed for short supplies of talent and capital. The Panic of 1893 vividly illustrated that both university investments and donors were at the mercy of economic fluctuations. And even nature could interrupt progress; Stanford's principal buildings fell in the earthquake of 1906.

The general trends in higher education resembled the search for direction and order in other walks of life. Academic planners rejected aristocratic British and classical French models, and turned to Germany, whose emphasis on science and specialization was appealing. A world shortage of experts sharpened the competition for faculty talent. University organizers like William Rainey Harper of Chicago, or Daniel Coit Gilman of Johns Hopkins exuded optimism, yet secured few distinguished foreigners. But new research facilities, and high salaries, increased faculty mobility at the top. A distinguished full professor might earn $5000, though beginners started closer to $1500, both appealing sums in untaxed gold dollars.

University leaders emphasized that research improved teaching and created a special tone that benefited faculty, students, and the community. The Harvard Overseers' report of 1869 established a luminous goal:

A university should give opportunity for universal culture; it should provide facilities in language, science, law, theology, medicine, engineering, architecture, and all the arts. It ought also to be furnished with museums, cabinets, libraries, botanic gardens, observatory . . . . By bringing together such varied apparatus for study, and so many teachers and students, a literary atmosphere is created as well as a tone of thought favorable to learning. Teachers have more of enthusiasm, and gain a larger, freer style of thought, in such a generous atmosphere. Pedantic narrowness is less likely to appear.[39]

The 'useful' preceded the arts, but the total performance registered in buildings, apparatus, enrollments, and degrees matched growth in other sectors of national life. And the educational system made long strides toward modernity and relevance.

The view from within a developing institution was often exciting. Professors had the sense of special community and attachment to world culture that animated painters and writers. With administrative cooperation, they established scholarly journals and learned societies. Universities sought distinguished foreign visitors, and supported expeditions to study Egyptology, anthropology, or meteorology. They cooperated with the national government and Smithsonian Institution to study flora and fauna, Indian life, and astronomy.

National associations of historians, economists, political scientists, and librarians appeared after 1875. Similar bodies staged conventions and published reports for engineers and scientists. Humanists wanted prestige and authority, but were typically American in seeking 'a better state of society than now exists'.[40] Conservatives feared the impact of skeptical science and depth research on established ideals. But the psychologist G. Stanley Hall summed up the excitement in trying to wed knowledge and progress:

We felt that we belonged to the larger university not made by hands, eternal in the world of science and learning; that we were not so much an institution as a state of mind and that wherever and to what extent the ideals that inspired us reigned, we were at home; that research is nothing less than religion; that every advance in knowledge today may set free energies that benefit the whole race tomorrow.[41]

Internal indexes of professional change seemed to omit

students. 'One is obliged to suspect, at times, that the student comes to be regarded as a mere disturber of ideal schemes, and as a disquieting element in what without him might be a fairly pleasant [faculty] life', President J. M. Taylor of Vassar College confessed in 1893.[42] As always, most young men went to college to gain earning power and escape parental control. Competition was keen within the educational system, and western schools like Michigan and California hoped to outshine 'conservative' Harvard. Johns Hopkins and Cornell were equally determined to eclipse Princeton and Yale. Ivy League schools generally represented the eastern middle and upper class. Growing western colleges took pride in democracy, and even in a touch of rawness. Most large student bodies represented the nation; Chicago's entering class of 1892 came from 33 states and 15 foreign countries.

Graduate students received excellent specialized instruction, and lower classmen benefited from President Charles W. Eliot's widely copied Harvard elective system that permitted students to choose courses around a central core of requirements. Engineering graduates increased from 2200 in the 1870s to over 10,000 in the 1890s. The number of doctors, dentists, lawyers, and industrial experts rose steadily. But most entering students wanted to teach. Of 3200 polled in 1897, 35 percent majored in literature and languages; 20 percent in history and the social sciences; 14 percent in pure sciences; 18 percent in philosophy and the fine arts; and 1 percent in mathematics.

Educational change altered women's economic status and freedom. In 1880, only 30 percent of colleges admitted women, and most attended special schools like Sarah Lawrence or Vassar. By 1900, the figure was at least 70 percent, and after 1903, Wabash College was the only midwestern college not to register women. Oracles and pundits manufactured jokes to illustrate growing female independence. A mythical girl wrote her father of receiving '100 in algebra, 96 in Latin, 90 in Greek, 88½ in mental philosophy,

and 95 in history; are you not satisfied with my record?'
The reply was not encouraging: 'Yes, indeed, and if your
husband happens to know anything about housekeeping,
sewing and cooking, I am sure your married life will be very
happy'.[43] But enrollments increased rapidly and education
helped mold social change. 'Men decry it, crack jokes about
it – and send their sons to college', a writer noted in 1905.[44]

Those who criticized the new learning's occasional shallowness overlooked its historic achievements, and missed the
essential point. A society that prized variety could not
divorce knowledge from life. '[It] spread everywhere the
most profound desire for culture and enlightenment', Hugo
Munsterberg said, 'and for this reason [has] been the necessary system for a people so informed with the spirit of self-
perfection'.[45] Given the task of incorporating world culture
and new knowledge into the American system, education
maintained a workable balance between aloof expertise and
social obligation, and promoted national unity.

Economic forces were a major factor in creating the fresh
sense of unity evident by 1900. They were most obvious in
corporate enterprise and a few large fortunes, but well-
being increased dramatically for most people. Concentrated
wealth shaped society less than an inevitable technological
revolution and mass-consumption. There was no denying
industrialism's costs, but the United States fared better than
most countries. Diversity, competing interests, and even the
confusion in using new ideas slowed the tendency toward
mass. Representative government and cultural pluralism
survived easily.

Nor were Americans especially materialistic. The human
desire for security and pleasure was universal; Americans
simply faced unusual choices. Increasing income and
expenditure were part of the national concern for mobility
and personal success. Money expanded individual freedom
and taste. And Americans who readily accepted technological changes were more often interested in convenience,
comfort, and personal expression than in mere possessions.

Critics correctly noted that neither impersonal forces nor human agents had spread prosperity evenly. Reformers urged greater use of government to maintain competition, and a body of regulatory legislation developed rapidly on both local and national levels in response to constituent pressures. But only a powerful central government armed with expertise unknown to the nineteenth century might have directed the total industrial process. No general demand created one; most Americans preferred the risks of competition to the inhibitions of bureaucracy. Given the country's diverse population, and the power of localism in human affairs, the economic and cultural stability evident in 1900 were remarkable.

As always, the old gave way slowly. Established attitudes and expectations gained force by representing security and order amid bewildering change. Answers to national problems required both the fact and the public sense of national unity and inter-dependence, which came only at the end of the century. A curious blend of apprehension and confidence marked the generation: apprehension at a sense of losing control over events, confidence that all would end well within the inherited ethic. By 1900, that success seemed assured, which reinforced the normal human tendency to seek accommodations within the existing system. The new industrial society revealed both immense achievements and unfinished tasks. But Americans had ample space and resources for further growth and experiment, and retained faith in the outcome of the unending process of making the United States a functioning nation and a viable culture.

[2]

The Politics of Nationalism

ON 5 March 1877, Rutherford B. Hayes became the nineteenth president of the United States, only the third
Republican to win the office. He came to the White House
after a tacit understanding that Reconstruction must end.
Though a militant Unionist, Hayes had long believed that
token force would never solve the vexing southern problem
for either blacks or whites. Like most Americans, he now
hoped that expanding material opportunity and relief from
political bitterness would close the sectional gap. The
federal government would aid the South with patronage
and internal improvements. Responsible southern whites
hopefully would insure Negro civil rights under the new
constitutional amendments and federal laws. As a former
governor of the key state of Ohio, Hayes also perceived that
Americans must face new problems rising from industrialism.

Hayes quickly fulfilled his pledge to remove the few
troops remaining in the last two 'unredeemed' states of
Louisiana and South Carolina. But while seeking sectional
tranquility, and hoping to move on to other questions,
Hayes and other moderate Republicans understood the
emotions behind an old abolitionist's remark: 'My judgement clearly approves the policy of Mr Hayes, yet my
feelings rebel. . .'.[1]

Critics accused the Republicans of abandoning the Negro,
but only a minority of dedicated 'Radicals' ever took up his
cause. Northern opinion had assumed in 1865 that federal
laws guaranteeing the Negro's personal safety and right to
vote would overcome his lack of skills and education. Radical
efforts to insure full equality failed because the public would
not support a complex long-term program of federal aid for

ex-slaves. Realistic politicians had to accept the public
mood. As a Radical Republican admitted: 'The North is
tired of the southern question, and wants a settlement, no
matter what.'[2]

As president, Hayes travelled widely to preach racial
coexistence and material uplift. His hope that the Unionist
'Old Whig' element would control southern affairs was
logical, but like most other people he misjudged the depth
of white opposition to racial equality. He wanted to build
a southern GOP on national issues that appealed to what
John Sherman called 'the producing classes, men who are
interested in industry and property'.[3] But Democrats did not
honor their part of the compromise of 1877; and the southern
Negro moved steadily into a subsidiary status that became
full segregation at the end of the century.

Hayes was determined not to be a mere figurehead, and
firmly protected his executive prerogatives, while trying to
broaden the Republican party's appeal. No scandal marred
his term; an exemplary personal life and apparent indifference to partisan abuse increased his popular appeal. By
being patient, respectable, and concerned with new issues,
Hayes gave his party a new record to build on.

His political task was not easy. Despite great sacrifices to
save the Union and abolish slavery, the Republican party
was young, and did not control a national majority. The
Democratic opposition revived in the 1870s by opposing
federal power, which seemed vastly increased since 1860.
Democrats commanded a formidable 'solid South', and
enclaves of voters in the Midwest and in northern cities that
made every presidential election uncertain. They were
usually able to thwart new departures in legislation. The
party's negativism and appeals to local pride unhappily
matched the general public mood after the frustrations of
Reconstruction.

The Democrats' ability to use localism under-scored the
country's uneasy transition from agrarian attitudes toward
the unifying tendencies of industrialism. Different customs

and economic activities in various sections were formidable obstacles to a national spirit and an integrated society. Midwesterners resented the old Northeast's power and cultural pretensions. The South seemed stagnant in a Union it could neither leave nor fully embrace. The West demanded assistance its population did not yet warrant. A steady influx of immigrants and sudden urbanization created new attitudes and needs, and at the same time enhanced the power of older ideas as people grew fearful of rapid change. The political system was not designed to answer such new problems quickly, even had solutions been apparent. Yet this same diversity produced fruitful compromises that promoted national stability.

These and other stresses and demands directly affected party politics. Hayes and other Republicans understood that the GOP could create a majority coalition and enact its nationalistic policies only by espousing doctrines that enfolded local demands and antagonisms. Yet they inherited a political system that had rested on bargains between powerful local leaders and national spokesmen. Tammany Hall and Alabama were both Democratic, yet had antagonistic desires; few leaders successfully appealed to the extremes they represented. Senator Roscoe Conkling of New York jealously guarded his local authority. He expected federal patronage and recognition from every Republican president, yet reserved the right to shape national policies and to choose presidential candidates.

Like all presidents, Hayes took a larger view. He supported moderate civil service reform both to improve the bureaucracy and to weaken semi-independent chieftains who threatened loyalty to the national party. Hayes' struggles with Congress involved more than an effort to enhance presidential authority. And debates over philosophy and method within each party marked the era's movement toward a functioning two-party system.

Public interest in national issues made politics an important force in promoting national unity. Foreign visitors marvelled at the ability of American audiences to sit through lengthy speeches on abstruse subjects like the silver question or tariff protection. In an era of balanced politics and rapidly changing constituencies, the individual voter was important, and participated in his party's contests. Henry Sienkiewiecz, Polish author of the best-selling *Quo Vadis?*, toured the United States in 1876–8. His initial surprise at egalitarian manners gave way to admiration for American mores and individual opportunities. He shrewdly perceived that the people who eagerly discussed public questions, 'simply through contact with politics or by direct participation in them not only acquire[d] certain information and attitudes, but also a wider knowledge and understanding of [their] environment.' The political arena was an informal schoolroom for the average American. 'He has heard about all of these things in school and read about them in the newspapers. He has had to think about them as a voter. He has heard a thousand political speeches, Republican and Democratic, in which everything was explained from all angles and virtually crammed into his head. His views may not always be profound; at times they may even betray an innate stupidity, but they will never reveal an absolute ignorance.'[4]

Issues and programs deeply concerned voters, but a pluralistic, mobile society required leaders whose lives and deeds transcended material success. The businessman never replaced the politician as a popular hero. Abraham Lincoln embodied the best of his party's ideals and of the American dream. Martyrdom made him a folk hero, the Great Emancipator and Savior of the Union. But he also popularized the idea of governmental assistance to ease life's basic inequities. While saving the Union, he never forgot its people. 'This is essentially a people's contest', he said in 1861. 'On the side of the Union, it is a struggle for maintaining in the world, that form, and substance of government, whose leading object is to elevate the condition of man – to lift artificial weights from all shoulders – to clear the paths of laudable pursuit for all – to afford all, an unfettered start, and a fair chance, in the race of life.'[5]

Though he lacked Lincoln's political skills, Ulysses S. Grant also embodied much of the American dream. He represented order and non-partisanship, which always appealed to Americans in confused times. With Lincoln's death, he symbolized nationalism, and helped stabilize the GOP while its other spokesmen sought to build a new majority coalition.

James G. Blaine was the rank-and-file Republican voter's *beau ideal*, and by the early 1880s worked hard to develop a new party majority. The most charismatic leader in national politics, Blaine created such intense reactions that wags said men went insane over him in pairs, one for and one against. Though he represented Maine, a small state faithful to the GOP, Blaine quickly developed a national viewpoint. He wanted to meet new industrial questions, and to forge a coalition of prosperous farmers, workers, and businessmen, all of whom would respond to the unifying nationalism in programs such as tariff protection. Blaine struggled to outwit fellow Republicans like Roscoe Conkling, who jealously guarded local power. Though fated not to win the presidency, Blaine was a major architect of Republican nationalism.

The tensions between politicians with national goals, and local leaders who especially feared presidential leadership, remained strong for a generation. But by the mid-1880s, a new kind of figure played an increasingly important role in wedding local interests and national aims. The diverse ethnic and economic interests in Democratic organizations like New York City's Tammany Hall were hard to fit into a national movement, especially in view of the Democracy's historic emphasis on states-rights. Republican politicians were more successful in blending local and national needs. Thomas Collier Platt, New York's 'Easy Boss' after Conkling's death, rewarded constituents with favors, but accepted the primacy of national Republican programs.

His state organization gave voters both material and emotional rewards, and he better understood his constituents
than did carping mugwumps. Even Theodore Roosevelt
perceived the sources of Platt's strength: his acceptance of
men's diverse values and expectations within an impressive
organization that enhanced the voter's sense of importance.
'Very many of Mr. Platt's opponents really disliked him and
his methods for esthetic rather than for moral reasons',
Roosevelt shrewdly noted, 'and the bulk of the people half-
consciously felt this and refused to submit to their leadership'.[6]

Platt's strength rested on the state's small towns and
countryside, while New York City remained the preserve of
the Democratic Tammany Hall organization. The premier
Republican urban leader sat in Philadelphia. Matthew
Stanley Quay avoided personalism by blending into the
ranks of followers he so carefully cultivated. The urbane,
intelligent Quay had many redeeming virtues. He fiercely
defended Indian rights, firmly advocated protection and
internal improvements, and had a national viewpoint that
fitted the needs and moods of the powerful Keystone State.

Opponents naturally pictured leaders like Platt and Quay
as baronial highwaymen, holding national administrations to
ransom, and ruling polyglot empires ruthlessly. They took
men as they found them, and knew the limitations of political action in defining and sustaining human rights and
privileges. But such leaders held their constituents with
services and recognition. The 'bosses' linked ideals and
programs to the masses they touched and respected. Their
organizations gave newcomers and settled Americans alike
a sense of belonging to an active party that represented the
producing classes.

Problems rising from the rapidly developing economy
inevitably replaced war issues. Most Americans accepted
the apparent logic of transferring the drive for equality from
legislation to economics. Material success might be more
progressive than laws. Republicans believed in individu-

alism, but assumed that government should promote and regulate economic matters that affected the whole nation. Tariff protection illustrated the party's concern for national development. Involving both emotional and tangible appeals, protection became the era's central public issue, and helped the Republicans gain a national constituency.

The existing tariff system dated from the Morrill Act of 1861, which closed the home market. But insatiable wartime demands drew in foreign goods while the domestic plant expanded. In peacetime much of the business community, agriculture, and labor opposed tariff reduction, hoping to cushion the home market during an expected transition to lower prices and production levels. This recession did not occur until 1873, and politicians then argued persuasively that protection had at least delayed the inevitable.

Popular spokesmen like Blaine and William McKinley effectively explained the complicated subject in national campaigns. The tariff aided mature establishments and fostered 'infant industries', while the economy could not meet foreign competition because of high wages paid to workingmen. In the home market, agriculture fed and clothed an expanding population. Protection also generated profits for reinvestment in a steady cycle of plant expansion and job development, which reduced dependence on foreign capital and diversified the economy. These basic arguments appealed to skilled workers, businessmen, and many farmers. The policy also involved strong emotions. It seemed suited to immediate needs and might stabilize an uncertain future; it was associated with great names like Alexander Hamilton, Henry Clay, and Abraham Lincoln.

General Hancock, the Democratic candidate for president, was essentially correct in calling the tariff a local issue during the campaign of 1880, but Republicans successfully combined local interests into a national appeal. Some Republicans favored selective downward revision, but congressional lobbying forbade 'scientific' management. Leaders had to accept some excessive rates, or endanger the whole system. Rutherford B. Hayes sounded a moderate but realistic note:

The practical question and the theoretical may be and usually are very different. My leanings are to the free trade side. But in this country the protective policy was adopted in the first legislation of Congress in Washington's time, and has been generally adhered to ever since. Large investments of capital, and the employment of a great number of people depend upon it. We cannot, and probably ought not to suddenly abandon it.[7]

Not all businessmen favored protection. Shippers and importers wanted selective lower rates; producers of some finished goods sought cheap foreign raw materials. A Massachusetts clothing manufacturer might lobby for free raw wool against fellow-Republican producers from Vermont, Ohio, and Wyoming. Only skillful party leadership harmonized these differences.

Critics charged that manufacturers increased profits by using the difference between cost and the tariff schedule as the retail price. The economics of the charge were hazy and statistics could 'prove' anything. American finished goods were expensive, but wages were higher than in Europe. Genuine free trade appealed to theoreticians who insisted that protection penalized consumers. But cheap English, Canadian, and Mexican goods would obviously invade an unprotected American market. And the 'consumers' who fascinated critics sold their skills in that market. As McKinley said, a jobless man could not buy cheap shoes. 'When prices were the lowest, did you not have the least money to buy with?'[8]

By the 1880s, protection drew many voters into the GOP in the industrializing states around the Great Lakes. Specialized farming increased rapidly there, involving poultry, dairy products, beef and mutton, and fruits and vegetables for city markets. These farmers liked the home market idea better than counterparts did in the wheat-producing West and cotton-bound South. They also feared the immediate threat of Canadian wheat, livestock feed, and wool. National legislators excluded fish, coal, and lumber from Canada; and hides, beef, wool, and ores from Mexico. Protection was as important to many farmers and raw material producers as to businessmen and workers. This combination of self-interest and emotional Americanism made the tariff a vital political issue.

Protection naturally had enemies. Many Democrats hoped to cast off their party's southern tone, and thus escape from the emotional war issues that kept them defensive. Tariff reform might enfold everyone who was hostile to industrialism. Reformers argued that protection raised prices without affecting wages, fostered monopolies, and hampered exports. These arguments reflected Democratic distrust of government. Trusts in oil and transportation did not benefit from protection. Demands for change also reflected hostility toward the East and uneven industrial expansion. And many genteel critics disliked congressional lobbying more than protection. Reform would weaken politicians, and begin the process of cleansing the government.

But the Democratic party was not united against protection. Samuel J. Randall of Pennsylvania led a bloc of congressmen who were Democratic on almost everything except the tariff and thwarted reformers until the late 1880s. Industrialism and production of diverse raw materials such as lumber, turpentine, coal, sugar, and citrus, increased the tariff's appeal in Border and southern states.

Republicans argued that protection fostered stability amid rapid expansion, and, in periodic slumps, opposed 'tariff tinkering' with equal effect. Illinois' crusty reformer William R. Morrison had a point in noting: 'The trouble with the tariff question is that the Republicans have the advantage on catch words, and the people as a rule do not understand the question, and it is too hard a study for them'.[9] But he did not explain why millions of voters read pamphlets, and attended long discussions of the subject. Or why the Democratic cry of 'lower taxes' took so long to impress voters.

The protective system had inequities, but it was a necessary part of unifying the American economy. It was probably
irrelevant to wheat and cotton producers, whose distress in
the 1890s stemmed from world overproduction. But it
helped heavy industry, fabrication, diversified farming, and
raw material production. It generated re-investment capital
through profits, and affected wages in important skills.
There was never any question that significant tariff reduction would open the home market to cheaper British goods.

As a major political issue, the tariff helped define men's
views of how the United States should develop, and the
parties offered voters a choice of policy. The Democrats
would not overturn the system, but President Cleveland's
proposed reforms of 1887 penalized raw material producers
and workers making finished goods. The changes would
have increased southern power, and were politically inspired to pacify staple-producing farmers, exporters, and
Democratic politicians seeking a unifying anti-industrial
issue. The question was equally important within both parties.
Republicans used the tariff to maintain a coalition of inter-
dependent but suspicious interests. And although the Democrats failed to reduce duties in the mid 1880s, by the end of
Cleveland's first term they began to unite on the theme of
lower taxes and less government aid to the economy.

The currency question revived while statesmen grappled
with the tariff schedules. From the days of Jackson's war on
the central bank, and the Lincoln administration's issuance
of greenbacks, Americans had argued bitterly over money's
form and function. 'There are as many financial sects in
America as there are parties in Spain', Henry Watterson
said.[10] The currency became a national problem because it
combined sectional, moralistic, and practical interests in a
knot that few politicians ever untied.

Demands to 'do something for silver' in the 1870s were
strong in the expanding Midwest. Business elements there,
whose eastern counterparts sought gold mono-metallism,
often wanted controlled inflation through an increasing

money supply that did not threaten bullion redemption. Many western bankers and businessmen found a certain insurance against the future in constant credit expansion. Agrarians believed they came last in the system's monetary priorities, since commercial enterprises were most attractive to investors. And men of all occupations in the South and West resented eastern political influence and cultural authority.

Debt was an emotional and practical part of the public's feelings, as contractual obligations appreciated during hard times. 'The suggestion that the silver dollar is a dishonest dollar is met with the statement that gold has appreciated, and to make the gold dollar the standard measure is to rob the debtor class for the benefit of the creditor class', William Henry Smith wrote President Hayes. 'Debts contracted when paper was at 80, 50, 20, and 10 per cent discount should not now be paid in gold – the effect with a single standard. This argument reaches the masses, and there is no effective way of answering it'.[11] The situation had ironies; a people devoted to profit still expected a certain leniency. Creditors who lent on shaky collateral had no right to excessive returns. And the recent wartime inflation that had alienated millions looked good during a depression. 'Our workingmen are captured with the proposition that when we had a great volume of depreciated currency in circulation, during and after the war, times were good and everybody had plenty of work,' a friend wrote Carl Schurz.[12] Wartime shortages, scarcity of labor, and expanding markets had created that prosperity. But many people only recalled the rustle of greenbacks when they lived in a buyer's market for credit. Yet millions of others did not want to check the dollar's relation to gold in the morning paper.

The Grant administration had flirted briefly with a contractionist policy that was popular among conservative bankers, but retreated quickly to a system of paper, silver, and gold. Republicans defeated efforts to adopt either 'rag money', or free coinage of silver. Lurid charges of conspiracy filled every debate over new legislation. Farmers saw a vast international 'gold-bug' conspiracy to defraud staple producers. Conservatives accused silverites of seeking a government purchase plan merely to bolster their declining business. But the desire for cheap dollars to pay fixed debts, for easy credit to underwrite commercial expansion, and sectional hostilities all underlay the pro-silver argument.

Most inflationists opposed non-redeemable paper currency, but put great faith in the silver dollar with 'intrinsic' value. People were familiar with 'cartwheels', and they could not pour from a printing press, which hopefully would control their inflationary effect. Yet Gresham's Law obviously operated. Few observers believed the United States could maintain an internationally recognized dollar on anything but a tacit gold standard, a significant point while American securities sold abroad. Gold was a critical part of the economic stability so important to a transitional generation: ' . . . the farmer's grain, the planter's cotton, the Chinaman's tea are all interchangeable on a common basis of value', an influential business journal said, 'and, as every venture is thus relieved of the elements of uncertainty, enterprise becomes less hazardous and therefore freer'.[13] As industrialism steadily triumphed, with imbalances and uncertainties, gold naturally acquired great stature as a symbol of national power and respectability.

An angry 'Greenback party' threatened Republican congressional strength in the Midwest, and the traditional compromise was in order. President Hayes vetoed the Bland-Allison Act of 1878, which provided for a limited number of new silver dollars. But Congress over-rode him, the dollars were minted, and the issue subsided with returning prosperity. Hayes's brilliant Secretary of the Treasury, John Sherman, met the 2 January 1879 deadline for redeeming greenbacks in gold.

The Bland-Allison measure did not fundamentally change the situation, and politicians hesitated to enact even larger futile subsidies. The world's great powers remained firmly

attached to gold, and a series of international conferences
failed to secure bi-metallism. Every major nation simply
wanted to give silver an elaborate public funeral. But
American silverites maintained influential propaganda
organisations, and had great power in the Senate. During
the hot summer of 1890, reluctant lawmakers adopted a
compromise purchase plan named for John Sherman, now a
senator from Ohio. The Treasury would buy 4,500,000
ounces of silver per month, the estimated national production. The Act did not threaten the tacit gold standard, but
laid up future trouble by paying for the bullion with new
Treasury Notes redeemable more than once 'in coin'. Every
administration assumed that this meant gold if the bearer
demanded it. No one guaranteed this compromise would
last any longer than that of 1878.

Few people understood the currency question's fiscal
details, and everyone labored under inadequate economic
theory. A centralized and flexible banking system, not more
currency, was the real need, but even the rashest statesman
shrank from reopening Jacksonian quarrels. Most politicians
saw periodic subsidy laws as bridges over depressions, effective until prosperity returned and dissipated public concern.
There was not much else to do, as Maine's realistic Republican Senator William P. Frye admitted candidly:

There is such a disagreement between men who ought to understand the financial questions that it makes one's brain buzz to read
their opinions. Since I have been in Congress, I have seen nearly
all of the predictions of financial men come to grief. I was here
throughout the refunding process, and every attempt to reduce the
rate of interest was declared to be dangerous; bonds would not be
floated at par at such low rates, etc., etc.; and yet we succeeded
every time in establishing a lower rate. When the Bland Bill was
passed, everybody seemed to think the price of silver would
increase, but it decreased. When the Sherman Bill became law,
we all knew that silver would appreciate rapidly, as that law provided for the purchase of the entire product; yet silver went down.
Now, where is wisdom to be found in these financial questions?
I am a bi-metallist, but I have very serious doubts about the

propriety of the United States going into free coinage alone. Of course, an international agreement would settle this thing, and if the horrors of gold mono-metallism are such as you describe, can other countries stand it any great length of time? Will not their eyes be opened as yours have been?[14]

Throughout these rancorous debates, Republican leaders sought workable compromises. While standing for 'sound money', they controlled critics with realistic purchase plans. The strong leadership of midwesterners like John Sherman and William McKinley reduced the appearance of eastern power in the GOP, and emphasized the party's nationalism. Republicans seemed responsible, yet flexible in meeting legitimate constituent demands; interested in controlling inflation, but mindful of the dollar's full symbolism. This stand appealed to the propertied middle class, to workers who feared inflation's effects on wages, and to diversified agrarians.

Politicians reared in the school of experience functioned reasonably well in legislating economic policy, but they were less successful in understanding the demand for civil service reform. The 'mugwumps', or erratic genteel reformers, threatened politicians' self-interest, and wrapped their own drive for power in a snobbish abstract reasoning. The typical mugwump believed in laissez-faire economics and small government. Residence in the burgeoning industrial cities jaundiced his view of the free ballot. The 'bosses' who controlled voters with patronage and government favors offended this gentry. Politicians taxed property to help 'the people', and the masses seemed indifferent to the 'corruption' that accompanied representative government, and disliked their 'betters'.

Like other marginal groups in the era's balanced and competitive party system, the genteel reformers had unusual power. As editors, professionals, and intellectuals, they commanded a significant audience through propaganda. Their gospel of efficiency appealed to some businessmen who mistakenly thought government was an enterprise. And through mugwump doctrine ran the unifying theme that 'spoilsmanship' bred paternalism and marked a decline from the pure ways of the fathers.

Awareness of their lessening importance in politics and society flavored much of the mugwumps' attack on patronage. They feared pluralism, and talked darkly of coming revolution if the masses were not curbed. A civil service resting on merit and tenure would be efficient, and act as a brake on free-wheeling politicians. Much of the indictment was worthwhile. But critics never understood the importance of patronage to the faithful Democrats or Republicans who discussed politics at city streetcorners and in country stores. Men who received office gained recognition in the community. Party organizations that offended mugwumps increased the average voter's standing.

Politicians answered reformers with a frank and appealing view of politics. The people wanted no impersonal government, however efficient. The threat of removal kept officials responsible to the electorate, and assessments on their salaries for campaign expenses were only fair. 'Every free government is necessarily a partisan government.'[15] Americans believed that partisan discussion was necessary to define and accommodate interest. Permanent tenure would breed arrogance in an unresponsive bureaucracy. Every man had a right to seek office as a reward for party service. And given the country's size and diversity, politicians needed 'spoils' to build and maintain their local organizations.

The politicians who were grappling with baffling new problems, and who were eager to recognize an ever-increasing electorate, did not agree that this reform would 'purify' politics. Opponents noted that mugwumps were 'progressive' only in seeking a more efficient government; they would not enlarge its functions. Yet the reformers were sometimes right for the wrong reason. In a period of rapid change that needed expertise, a merit civil service might help to rationalize growth. Only orderly administration could expand government operations, an irony that most reformers missed while seeking retrenchment.

President Hayes accepted the need for civil service reform, and stubbornly fought fellow Republicans, even at the risk of party rupture. He wanted to abolish assessments and to appoint meritorious partisans, but foes understood his larger design. 'We must limit and narrow the area of patronage.', he said privately. 'We must diminish the evils of office seeking. We must stop interference of federal officers with elections. *We must be relieved of congressional dictation as to appointments.*'[16] Hayes obviously intended to maintain executive authority, and to nationalize his party's appeal.

He did not reform the service, but set a precedent no successor could easily ignore. In 1880, both parties depended on office-holders for campaign funds, and straddled the issue. As an experienced congressman, the Republican candidate James A. Garfield was skeptical of the mugwump shibboleth. 'No phase of it would stand the schoolmasterish examinations and the absurd attempt to get on without the aid of congressmen in making selections,' he privately wrote Blaine. 'I believe in party government, and that the spirit and doctrines of the Republican party should prevail in the executive departments.'[17]

But as president, Garfield quickly accepted Hayes's idea. From March 1881, until his assassination in July, he fought and defeated Senator Conkling as an object lesson to local leaders. He also accepted civil service as part of stabilizing politics. His tragic death in September popularized the cause, though a comprehensive law did not come until 1883.

The Pendleton Act bore an Ohio Democrat's name, indicating consensus on the need for expertise in government. Congressmen also could not spend every day worrying over minor appointments. The Act outlined a system expandable at presidential will, that avoided sectionalism and elitism. Entrance to the limited 'classified service' depended on examination, but both practical experience and book learning counted. 'This bill assumes that every citizen has an equal claim to be appointed if he has equal capacity', Dorman B. Eaton, a leading reformer, assured critics.[18]

Reformers did not secure the rudimentary merit system alone. Ranking politicians wished to nationalize politics and improve government. The tenacious efforts of Presidents Hayes and Garfield to realign GOP loyalties and policies enfolded civil service reform. Like all landmark legislation, the Pendleton Act was bi-partisan, but it redounded to Republican credit, and illustrated the ability of GOP leaders to secure workable compromises.

Despite its importance to politicians and reformers, civil service attracted less voter attention than veterans' pensions, internal improvements, and taxation. In 1876, the government spent about one tenth of its budget on pensions; in 1886, the total was one fourth. The Grand Army of the Republic promoted veterans' demands, and Congress passed thousands of bills for claimants whom the Pension Bureau rejected.

Veterans' benefits were important to many able and honest men who feared that a new generation would forget the war's full cost and purpose. Nothing was too good for a Union soldier. As late as 1889, with an omnibus pension bill pending, ex-President Hayes voiced this fighting spirit:

> The rich, the well-to-do, and those who depend mainly on them, are strangely blind as a class to what is due – in short, to justice to the Union soldier. Bonds for money lent the government in paper, worth thirty-five to sixty-five cents on the dollar, are paid in gold at their face value, with gold interest at highly remunerative rates. *That* national obligation, I, with you and the rich people, insisted upon because it was just. But the men paid twenty or thirty cents a day for life and uncounted sacrifices are said to make a 'raid upon the Treasury' if they ask that promises be kept.[19]

He would have agreed with Wisconsin's Republican Senator Philetus Sawyer who saw pensions as relief for the poor and distressed who had risked more than the rich. 'The money will get into circulation and come back to the Treasury', he said, and thought that officials should pass a shaky claim rather than risk being unjust.[20]

Republicans saw these benefits as one way of funding the national economy, but Democrats charged that such expenditures were merely a way to reduce the treasury surplus and avoid tariff reform. This attitude also thwarted federal spending for education. Four times during the 1880s, Senator Henry W. Blair of New Hampshire piloted through one branch of Congress a bill to give federal money to the states on an illiteracy formula that would benefit chiefly the South. This was a logical extension of the Republican Morrill Act of 1862, which granted public domain to state universities. But fears of federal authority, and the straw man of racial integration combined with local pride to defeat the measure.

The GOP also favored early statehood for western territories, with generous subsidies for public facilities that aided their developing economies. Lawmakers expanded mail service, improved communications, and used the army to maintain order and spend money. By the 1890s, an enlarged Agriculture Department distributed seeds and expert advice to farmers. Internal improvements, tariff protection, and a sense of national attachment finally over-rode free silver to make most western states Republican.

But the practice of federal subsidy was inevitably uneven, and by the late 1880s, many farmers resented assistance to the industrial sector. Democrats opposed spending and played on fears that the central government would regulate personal life. But Republicans did not employ subsidies merely to enrich a few, or to buy votes. The trans-continental railroad, river and harbor improvements, and public facilities were national responsibilities that enlarged the scope of individual opportunity. And subsidies were not to be permanent, but would aid only the first stages of growth.

The weakness of this materialistic view, which matched the country's historic ethic, lay in the lack of supervision in a nation too large for indirect control. But when demands for regulation crystallized in the late 1880s, Republicans led in securing expandable measures like the ICC Act of 1887, and the Sherman Antitrust Act of 1890. They showed a keen understanding of American diversity, which required balanced policies that would not jeopardize the whole by penalizing some interests.

These successful compromises in economic policies did not carry over to the unhappy race question. The great majority of Negroes were isolated in the South, invisible to most Americans, and at the mercy of local interests. The electorate never supported the Radical Republican program of protected civil rights that was necessary for the freedman's safety and progress. The bitterness and long duration of an apparently fruitless Reconstruction made voters reject further sacrifices for the Negro. As a new generation came of age, economics replaced the long-debated race question. The Negro's aspirations remained the great unfulfilled part of the American dream.

Yet most Americans believed in the free ballot. The tariff question dominated the boisterous campaign of 1888, but Benjamin Harrison typified those who believed in racial justice, and warned that he would try to protect voting rights under the Fifteenth Amendment. 'The Republican party has always stood for election reforms', he told a campaign crowd. 'No measure tending to secure the ballot box against fraud has ever been opposed by its representatives.'[21] Voting guarantees would help Republican candidates in the South, but the question was basically moral for Harrison. 'I would not be willing myself to purchase the presidency by a compact of silence upon this question', he wrote privately.[22]

Partisanship was naturally involved in demands for federal supervision of elections. Republican presidents since Hayes had accepted 'black and tan' parties in the South, but rewarded Negroes with patronage and recognition. They argued realistically that any GOP organizations were

better than no contrast at all to sterile one-party politics.
Increased Negro voting would help local Republican candidates. Southern states would not support Republican presidential candidates, but by 1890, some districts might elect
Republican congressmen as industrialization sharpened the
appeal of tariff protection.

Intangibles were equally important. A rising nostalgia
about the war and its results alarmed Republicans in the
late 1880s. An 'Old South' myth sprang up, in which happy
slaves sang in the cotton fields, and every family had a
plantation home which the yankees burned. Jefferson Davis
became a twilight hero, and Stephen Foster's maudlin songs
dominated music halls. Elaborate jubilees reminded southern
veterans of a 'Lost Cause', which Unionists had called simple
treason. And violence at the polls revealed an increasing
southern determination to prevent Negroes from voting.

When the Fifty-first Congress assembled in December,
1889, Representative Henry Cabot Lodge of Massachusetts
introduced a new voting rights measure. He tried to avoid
the bogey of military rule by providing for careful appeal
to the federal courts. But southerners labelled the measure a
'Force Bill', and Lodge drew fire from others who resented
its national scope. Machine bosses did not want watchful
federal courts. The growing Farmers' Alliance feared integration, and any increased Republican strength. Mugwumps disliked enlarging the electorate. Some labor
leaders like Terence V. Powderly feared even potential use
of troops. And many northern businessmen opposed anything
that might provoke southern boycotts.

This hostility aroused intense feeling among Republicans
who remembered the quest for social justice that followed
saving the Union. Senator William E. Chandler of New
Hampshire said that no one could resist voting rights and
be in the GOP. 'His only proper place is with the Negro-
baiting, Republican-killing Democracy.'[23] Calmer men
shared that reaction, but as usual, Senator Sherman realistically analyzed the question:

I appreciate as fully as you do the importance of maintaining
and encouraging the good will, harmony and reciprocity now
existing between the North and the South, and dislike to vote for
any measure that may, in the opinion of men like yourself, tend to
renew sectional excitement and controversy. But what can we do?
Here it is alleged and apparently admitted that more than a
million of lawful voters are substantially disfranchised by the
Democratic party where their votes would change the result; that
not only are they denied political rights, but the political power
awarded to them is used against them; that in this way gross
inequality of representation in Congress is made in favor of the
South, so that the vote of one Democrat in the South is equal to
two or three Republicans in the North. Now is it strange that we
should feel this is an injustice that ought not to be inflicted by the
South or tolerated by the North; that we ought if possible to
secure a free and fair election of members of Congress, so that all
citizens may have an equal vote, and have their votes counted?[24]

Southerners also understood that a Republican Congress
could negate obstructive state voting laws if it enacted
Lodge's bill.

Despite heated debate, the proposal was doomed. It
passed the House by a strict party vote, then became embroiled in silver and tariff legislation in the Senate. Fanatical
silverites forced leaders to carry it over or lose the tariff bill,
and killed it in the short session that followed the congressional elections. 'This is but another sign that the inevitable
is coming', a friend wrote Senator Sherman, 'and the people
are more interested in the money matters than in election
bills.'[25] Perhaps, but the defeat rankled those who did not
think free silver was a cure-all for man's ills, or the proper
trade for a free ballot. In 1894, the Cleveland administration repealed all federal election laws, a stark illustration of
party differences.

The great body of nationalistic doctrine which Republicans enacted into policy after 1861 did not go unchallenged.
The cost of federalism, deeply rooted localism, and fear of
government kept the nation's tone Democratic long after
that party's programs and ideas had lapsed. Democrats had

a rhetorical commitment to the 'common man', and symbolic heroes. Only Lincoln rivalled Jefferson and Jackson in the nation's pantheon. If the GOP failed to transform the United States, as many predicted, he would endure merely as the great spokesman of a third party that failed.

Democratic negativism appealed to voters who suspected government and disliked taxation. In national affairs, the party's 'Solid South' produced disproportionate congressional strength, and automatically put its presidential candidate in sight of success. Ethnic groups scornful of Republican 'respectability' formed the basis of Democratic power in some northern cities. Democratic businessmen and professionals preached laissez-faire ideas, and feared that government might interfere with individualism.

Whatever its diverse following, the Democracy stood everywhere for localism, the self-help myth, and racial inequality. No Republican believed in an uncontrolled marketplace as fervently as did Grover Cleveland. Much of this attitude derived from wartime experience with federal regulations, the draft, and high taxes. The effort to secure Negro rights alienated most Democrats, including urban immigrants who did not want to compete with blacks for jobs or status. But Democrats simply had a historical aversion to government. Governor William E. Russell of Massachusetts typified the view that government was 'a power to protect and encourage men to make the most of themselves, and not something for men to make the most of.'[26] Ranking Democrats often praised a style of rugged individualism that never existed. After a trip to the Great Lakes, Delaware's conservative Senator Thomas F. Bayard thanked his host for lessons in life and economics:

I can still shut my eyes and see the stately procession of majestic vessels, freighted with the native products of the vast Mid-west, moving noiselessly along the pathway of beneficent exchanges. What a lesson is here against governmental interference! How wisely the well-instructed spirit of self-interest works in self-

directed channels, and is developed by natural competition without fear of contact with malificent [*sic*] statutes![27]

This was a fantasy, of course. No area had benefited more
from federal assistance than the Midwest. Tariff protection,
expanded federal services, and subsidies for waterways,
lakefront developments, public facilities, and railroads had
all hastened the area's growth.

Republicans accepted the logic of local control of local
affairs, but only in an integrated economy and in a society
with nationalistic ideals. The centralized promotion and
regulation they espoused was still new. It took a full generation of intense debate and example to make it seem comfort-
able to a majority of voters.

Democrats were united only in presidential campaigns, or
in the occasional congressional year involving an over-
riding issue. But their quadrennial search for a harmony
candidate was difficult, since localism did not produce
national figures. The Democrats could not afford southern
leadership, or any overt spokesman of the Northeast. They
solved the problem only once with New York's Grover Cleveland. He repeated the accepted platitudes, but really won in
1884 with luck, apparent independence from his own party,
and by standing for retrenchment. Between 1885 and 1889,
Cleveland shrewdly cultivated an image of aloofness from
sordid politicking and used lofty rhetoric to cover the cracks
in this party's unity and purpose.

The office Cleveland held was not overtly powerful. The
president symbolized the nation and fulfilled his minimal
constitutional duties. He also distributed patronage and
recommended legislation, but it was a time of party development, with little room for dramatic executive pressure. A
president could exhort, influence, and persuade, but congressmen did not tolerate dictation. A president's chief
public role was ceremonial, to foster nationalistic loyalties
and to sustain democratic egalitarianism. Citizens who
assumed they had a natural right to visit an unguarded chief
executive at the White House, considered any president

undemocratic who sought to mobilize public opinion on any but the loftiest question. The president's public role produced largely symbolic authority which only the most astute politician like William McKinley could transform into political leverage.

But presidents guarded their prerogatives. Even the mild Hayes beat Congress on points of honor and policy involving executive power in dealing with the army and appointments. Yet no president increased his authority with dramatic appeals to the public, though Hayes, Garfield, and McKinley were especially astute in employing subordinates. These leaders simply lacked the party unity and secure electoral base to risk drama.

Presidential campaigns, however, were great events. Candidates had to typify American ideals, discuss present issues, and at least outline the future. The electorate loved oratory, but no generation absorbed more information on complex questions through both the printed and spoken word. Individual voters were important in close contests. A high proportion balloted, indicating interest in issues and attachment to party. Only Grant and McKinley won national popular majorities, though the electoral count was in doubt but once, in 1876. And alternating party control of one or both houses of Congress inhibited dramatic action. The Democrats captured the House eight of ten sessions between 1875 and 1895. Republicans usually organized the Senate only by narrow margins because of the violent silver question. The GOP actually controlled Congress with safe majorities only after 1899, when 'McKinley prosperity' and pride in overseas expansion ended the currency question.

Yet for all their confusion, presidential campaigns were important in the long process of intra-party alignment, and for defining issues between the parties. In 1880, the GOP chose a classic dark horse from Ohio, James A. Garfield. His defeat of General Grant's bid for a third nomination indicated a turn from war issues to economic questions. General

Winfield Scott Hancock, the Democratic candidate, also symptomized a halting urge among leaders to seek unity and a new direction with an aloof military figure. The returns revealed a 'solid South', but Garfield's election indicated the GOP's ability to survive with new leadership. Equally significant, tariff protection appealed widely. Garfield's tragically brief term was also important, since with Blaine's help, he defeated Roscoe Conkling as an object lesson to other leaders who threatened national authority. Garfield's death left the GOP in a kind of limbo at just the moment when he might have used his new popularity to enhance the appeal of unifying national issues. Chester A. Arthur had no mandate, and despite a good legislative record, became the only incumbent president unable to secure his party's renomination.

That reward passed to James G. Blaine, clearly the popular choice of most Republicans in 1884. The tarnished campaign, featuring Blaine's alleged corruption and Cleveland's sex life, obscured the continuing trend toward nationalistic politics. Blaine broke precedent and toured the Midwest and Northeast, stressing the virtues of economic legislation. His narrow defeat was not so striking as his near success. He won 400,000 more votes than Garfield had in 1880, helped enlarge the Republican congressional delegation, and enhanced national party loyalty.

Cleveland consistently posed as an efficient executive, immune to partisan appeals, which made him look better than his discordant party. But he did not enlarge the Democracy, and in 1887 gambled that a dramatic call for tariff reduction would re-elect him. Though Cleveland emphasized the non-partisan nature of an appeal for lower taxes, political needs dictated the move. Party leaders convinced the President that the issue would overcome the Democracy's southern image, and appear relevant to industrial problems. Properly managed, the demand for reduction would create a loose crusade of everyone with a grievance against the changes that industrialism produced.

This would neutralize the silver question, on which Democrats always sharply divided.

The plan had superficial political appeal, but success required careful organization, which Democrats always disliked, and presidential tact, which Cleveland lacked. The Mills Bill of early 1888 also combined the worst features of southern and northeastern localism. Its provisions for free wool, hides, ores, and lumber angered raw material producers. Republicans called it the first step toward free trade, proof that Democrats could not govern an industrial society. This charge appealed strongly to skilled workers in doubtful states, and Cleveland retreated. He privately sought a modified protectionist platform at the party's convention, and then angered reformers by refusing to campaign or to explain adequately the reform issue. His hesitations illustrated the dangers in presidential appeals.

Republicans countered with a unity candidate from the crucial Midwest, Benjamin Harrison of Indiana. Though his independence later angered GOP leaders, in 1888 he stressed the virtues of party loyalty and tariff protection. Republicans employed intense local organization, popular participation in a 'front-porch' campaign, and pamphlets and speakers. Businessmen paid most of the bills, but despite lurid charges of 'frying the fat' from protected interests, the tariff was not a one-constituency issue. Skilled workers and prosperous farmers voted for Harrison. He received a firm electoral majority, but fewer popular votes than Cleveland, who won increased tallies in one-party southern states.

The new administration's narrow control of Congress set the stage for an extraordinary session. Between 1889 and 1891, Republican leaders secured a compromise silver purchase bill, an anti-trust law, and the McKinley Tariff, with an important reciprocity system. But they also spent lavishly on pensions and internal improvements. The nation as a whole voted for protection in 1888, but not for a higher tariff, and probably expected Harrison to reduce taxation. In the bitter congressional elections of 1890, Democrats drummed the themes of government spending and tariff inequities. Republicans were also embroiled in explosive local contests concerning sabbatarian laws, school curricula, and temperance reform. The Democrats won the House, and Harrison was a lame-duck.

The President would clearly lose in 1892, but he gained renomination as a matter of pride. Ex-President Cleveland won a third nomination as the champion of tariff reform. Astute managers billed Cleveland as a reformer who would reward agrarians who distrusted his conservative allies. Cleveland secured 400,000 more votes than Harrison, in the first presidential election in which all states employed the Australian ballot. He won 277 electoral votes to the President's 145, and the Democrats controlled both House and Senate. If they maintained prosperity and convinced voters that tariff reduction would affect other aspects of life, the Democrats might enjoy a long lease on power.

But a few shrewd analysts warned Cleveland of the disruptive potential in agrarian unrest. Farmers near urban centers, and in specialized production, appreciated the new consumer economy. But western and southern producers of wheat, cotton, and livestock were not benefiting from industrialism as much as workers or businessmen. The collapse of a speculative western land boom, over-production, and increasing world competition in the late 1880s produced a 'Populist Revolt'.

Farmers lacking easy access to urban markets could not organize a multitude of small production to affect prices. Southerners tilling small plots, and westerners eager to expand their acreage both suffered from a credit system that favored industrial investment. Though hardly radical, discontented agrarians sought more regulation of transportation and the currency supply, and some special programs. Their fierce rhetoric delineated both material grievances against the centralizing economy, and resentment at urban attitudes that were replacing the rural verities in national mythology.

Few farmers were ready to abandon old party allegiances, though a Peoples' Party candidate sought the presidency in 1892. His poor showing outside areas producing wheat, silver, and cotton briefly reassured regular politicians. But farmers were over-represented in the balanced political system, and hard times might permit Populists to form a coalition of all those dissatisfied with industrialism.

Cleveland was completely unsuited to the delicate and complex task of balancing these tendencies. Events intensified his narrow view of politics and isolation from the people. The economy collapsed in April 1893; gold hoarding and evaporating credit warned of failing confidence in the complicated fiscal system. The President's advisers, chiefly eastern businessmen and bankers, and southern conservatives, thought that fresh public confidence would prevent a financial panic from becoming an industrial depression. Cleveland agreed. He would save the gold standard at all costs, and repeal the Sherman Silver Purchase Act as a gesture necessary to restore confidence.

The plan was economically inadequate and politically fatal. Cleveland used his personal influence and patronage in the most ruthless manner, and when he signed the repeal bill on 1 November 1893, the Democratic party was shattered. The groups that looked beyond tariff reduction departed, and Populists hoped to gather bitter men who could not find a job or sell their produce. Appearances counted against Cleveland, who now seemed to represent only the rich and the Northeast. Between 1893 and 1896, in contrast, Republican leaders first accepted bi-metallism, then 'sound money', and finally the gold standard as party doctrine. This realistic moderation looked good beside Cleveland's simplistic financial views.

The Democratic Congress immediately went from the abrasive silver question to tariff reduction, which Cleveland thought would restore party harmony. But the public opposed 'tariff tinkering' during a depression, and the Democrats were no more united on that issue than on anything else. The protectionist Wilson-Gorman Tariff did not redeem the campaign pledge of 1892. Republicans justly said it was sectional, that it proved the tariff's general virtues, and that they could do it better. Cleveland bitterly assailed lieutenants for failing to obtain further downward revision, and let the bill become law unsigned. This was only one of many displays of presidential contempt that infuriated fellow Democrats who had sacrificed a great deal for Cleveland in 1892.

The legislative fiasco of 1893-4 proved to most voters that the Democracy could not meet a crisis. Under the impact of events, it fell into naturally antagonistic component parts. Cleveland did not cause the depression, but his unnecessarily heavy-handed approach to meeting it made Republicans shine by contrast. Their historic record was more progressive, and they now seemed attuned to national needs.

These events and frustrations signalled bitter and significant off-year elections in 1894. Prominent Republicans like Thomas B. Reed sounded the keynote. 'Prosperity does not perch upon uncertainty; it can never ripen fruit as long as these noisy boys are clubbing the tree.'[28] In the Midwest, Republicans rallied to ex-President Harrison's text: 'We were told in the old times that the rich were getting richer and the poor poorer; and to cure that imaginary ill, our political opponents have brought on a time when everybody is getting poorer.'[29] Governor William McKinley of Ohio was the season's hero. Capitalizing on widespread personal popularity and identification with protected prosperity, McKinley conducted a vivid campaign for local Republican candidates. He could not fulfill 2500 invitations to speak, but appeared 371 times in 16 states.

The results were not surprising. Only 104 Democrats would face 245 Republicans in the new House, and the GOP had a slender majority in the Senate. In 24 states, no Democrat won federal office; 6 others chose only 1 each. 'Honey Fitz' Fitzgerald of Boston was the lone Democratic congressman from all of New England. The President was almost universally hated; the wrecked Democracy was adrift. The GOP at last looked like the majority party.

The new People's Party shared in the disaster, gaining no significant working-class or urban strength. Workers clearly wanted tariff protection, and distrusted agrarian rule. A third party victory was most unlikely; in hard times, voters turned to familiar Republican programs. GOP spokesmen were clearly more attuned to change than Democrats, and far better able to govern than Populists.

The elections outlined a coming GOP triumph in 1896, and made William McKinley the country's best known politician. Geography and experience were not his only claims on the party. He travelled widely and understood the whole nation better than most northeastern Republicans or Democrats. His midwestern origins, personal fulfillment of the American style, and talent for constructive compromise were formidable recommendations. He believed in the social rewards of success, and wanted to expand the system for everyone. He was a master politician among professionals, but did not forget either the desires or limitations of the turbulent electorate.

McKinley matured in the hard school of Ohio politics which mirrored the nation in microcosm. The varied needs of sellers and shippers, farmers and workers, miners and investors, professionals and merchants kept his district uncertain. But in a country of conflicting but interdependent interests, a safe district was fatal to aspirants for national office. Only a man who learned to compromise could lead. McKinley's new title, 'The Advance Agent of Prosperity', seemed both accurate and compelling to voters who trusted his moderate record and plans.

In January 1896, McKinley concluded two terms as governor of Ohio, and retired to his home in Canton to organize a campaign. Accepting the time-honored fiction that presidential hopefuls did not publicly seek the office, he let Marcus A. Hanna manage the cause. A wealthy Cleveland industrialist, Hanna had worked for Senator Sherman before transfering his intense personal loyalty to McKinley. To avoid political liens, he personally spent over $100,000 on 'The Major's' cause. A corps of silent, efficient aides arranged for speakers, literature, and local organizations while McKinley dealt with the press and politicians.

As a midwesterner, McKinley was slightly suspect to conservative Republicans, and to chieftains like Platt and Quay. Hanna capitalized on the slogan 'The People Against the Bosses', and defeated 'favorite son' candidates at state conventions. By June 1896, McKinley clearly would win a first ballot nomination.

McKinley quietly engineered a gold plank in the platform, but hoped to de-emphasize the currency question. The unexpected nomination of William Jennings Bryan upset Republican plans for a tariff campaign. The attractive young Nebraskan touted free silver as a panacea for all the nation's ills, and toured in a special train, speaking over 600 times in nearly every state. The defection of Silver Republicans limited McKinley's prospects in the West. The Populists endorsed Bryan, and bolting Gold Democrats further complicated the situation.

The drama around Bryan's under-dog campaign alarmed GOP managers, who feared the effects of any crusade in hard times. But McKinley shrewdly refused to imitate Bryan's new whirl-wind style. He remained at home, speaking to varied delegations, while Hanna's superb organization flooded the country with literature and speakers. McKinley became the calm and rational statesman amid shallow hurly-burly, stressing the general themes of unity and broadened opportunity under a safe and respectable Republican administration. While emphasizing protection, he promised to seek an international silver agreement. The heart of his argument was a clear realization that Bryan's agrarian constituency could not govern an industrial country.

Bryan's one-issue campaign faltered in October. More and more people doubted his ability, and distrusted his

motley followers. On election day, McKinley won the belt
of states from Minnesota to Maine, and Kentucky, West
Virginia, Oregon, and part of California's tally, for 271
electoral votes to Bryan's 176. He was the first candidate
since Grant to win a popular majority, but it was not a
landslide. Although the GOP captured control of the
House, the Senate was badly fragmented. Only the new
president's extraordinary political skill could manage
Congress.

The results confirmed the long-term trends forecast in
1894. The GOP triumphed on its past record, present
proposals, and obvious ability to represent an industrial
constituency. When an opaque anti-imperialism joined free
silver in the Democratic campaign of 1900, the President
easily won re-election, with firm control of Congress.

The contests of 1896 and 1900 marked the establishment
of an electorate oriented toward industrial rather than
agrarian authority. By the end of the century, responsible
two-party government was at last a fact of national life, and
would provide the means to expand government services in
accordance with the popular will. Politics also gave individual voters a strong sense of identity with national
problems, and was a major factor in creating national unity.

[3]
The Search for a National Culture

The Union triumph impressed foreigners, although many doubted that the United States could maintain cultural pluralism. But the country's absorption of new population, technical sophistication, and economic growth soon prompted uneasy talk of 'an American menace' abroad. The Republic's alleged unique qualities alternately amused and fascinated visitors. Charles Dickens and Matthew Arnold found a nation of rustics, but more acute tourists were impressed with America's achievements and future prospects.

Americans were always quick to display and praise material gains and innovations. They took immense and often annoying pride in democratic manners, individual successes, and collective power. But their eagerness for approval also struck visitors. Beneath aspersions against the 'Old World', and a constant striving for improvement, Americans felt culturally inferior. Machines, buildings, developing territories were tangible, but would the United States ever replace conservative Europe without developing a distinctive culture? Early nationalists had often equated art with decadence and aristocracy. But by mid-century, more and more Americans became aware of their country's cultural achievements, and of world tastes and affairs. The arts ceased to seem snobbish, and became badges of respectability. They were also an important part of continuity and progress. Culture could combine idealism and power, while developing the individual's 'higher' faculties. A good standard of living was not enough for supposedly materialistic Americans.

The United States had produced more art than its people realized, but communication and the pull of Europe dissi-

pated its presence. The country's size, variety, and regional
styles weakened resistance to world tastes that seemed to fit
changing national needs. Like diplomacy and politics, the
arts registered both the unifying tendencies of world developments, and disruptive new ideas. Improved communications
and an inter-dependent world community promoted 'a free
trade in ideas, resulting in a kind of cosmopolitanism. . .'.[1]

This internationalism briefly revived the debate over
whether Americans should seek unique art forms, or adapt
traditional approaches. Throughout the industrializing
western world, artists embraced new esthetic views at a time
when established formulas were tenacious because of their
comforting attachments to the past. Creative Americans
adopted many cosmopolitan tastes without abandoning a
unique and valuable angle of vision. The American artist's
role was never easy, but his task was no harder than that of
counterparts elsewhere. And while public receptiveness to
innovation enhanced eclecticism, it also prevented the
triumph of a reigning dogma. Painters, poets, and writers
complained of public indifference and academic hostility,
but every idea had a hearing. A healthy individualism and
variety permeated the arts, and the number of people who
cared for culture steadily increased. 'However little our
people know about Art', a critic noted in 1867, 'they are
eminently *teachable*'.[2]

New public libraries in most towns displayed current
periodicals and books of all kinds. Major cities built central
libraries and served a larger constituency through branches.
Expanding universities accumulated books, and public
agencies established special collections. The federal government aided the Smithsonian Institution, and bought
materials for specialized scientific studies. The lavish and
carefully planned Library of Congress, finished in 1897,
typified the desire to organize and expedite the flow of
information.

Post-war writers saw a radically changed literary landscape. The decline of the Boston Brahmins indicated that

literature had to reflect national variety and develop new unifying themes. Those themes were diverse. The revolution in magazine production created an insatiable market for serialized historical costumery and sentimental love stories. Yet, such writing often depicted urban life to rural readers, and analyzed new social situations. 'Pulp' magazines and dime novels also satisfied interest in the West, the cities, and the success ideal. Most news-stands and country stores had a shelf of Horatio Alger books, whose appeals were more complex than their rags-to-riches plots revealed. The narratives emphasized luck as the central element of success for the young man courageous enough to seize the main chance. And their fast pace and child protagonists appealed to young readers, who relished exotic surroundings and skulduggery.

An outpouring of inexpensive technical works accelerated the flow of ideas and information. Simplified manuals and periodicals helped laymen grapple with many of industrialism's mundane challenges. Travel books, home-planning guides, art portfolios, and educational material testified to increasing literacy and broadening taste.

In the realm of creative fiction, William Dean Howells linked industrial America to her rustic past. A prolific writer of novels, reviews, and criticism, he encouraged scores of aspiring authors even when disliking some of their work. Howells was born on the Ohio frontier, and prized humanistic values, but both as a man and an artist he understood the changes at work in his era. A collection of essays entitled *Criticism and Fiction* (1891) defined a literary Realism that rested on observable fact. Howells argued that 'what is unpretentious and what is true is always beautiful and good, and nothing else is so'.[3] He disliked variations from the norms of human behavior and social situations, whether in costumery or romance. 'Men are more alike than unlike one another', he insisted, '[so] let us make them know one another better, that they may be humbled and strengthened with a sense of their fraternity'.[4]

Howells filled his novels with the details of everyday life,
and also employed the international setting to analyze
changing customs and ideals. But decor only highlighted a
concern for individual responses to events and other people.
Realism was an effort to understand America's new codes of
conduct and social settings. Two of his best novels dealt
directly with the impact of industrialism on inherited
morality. *The Rise of Silas Lapham* (1885) depicted a newly
rich businessman who refused to abandon humanistic values
for profit. In *A Hazard of New Fortunes* (1890), Howells
shrewdly analyzed the effects of wealth and changing status
on several characters. The best chapters detailed a clash
between business power and trade unionism, and the stresses
involved in adapting individualistic ethics to a complex and
impersonal urban life.

Despite his apparent gentleness, Howells espoused many
social reforms. He attacked the patently unfair trials of the
Haymarket anarchists; discussed the taboo of divorce in *A
Modern Instance* (1882); and advocated prison reform and
women's suffrage. *A Traveler From Altruria* (1894), and
Through the Eye of the Needle (1907) outlined human equality
in a utopian society that rested on Christian cooperation.
Howells was pre-eminently an artist, but he placed both his
viewpoint and material at the service of a society seeking
unity and direction.

Samuel Langhorne Clemens was among Howells's life-
long friends. Fame and fortune followed the publication of
The Innocents Abroad (1869), and 'Mark Twain' needed no
introduction to a people whose mercurial temperament he
often symbolized. His nervous willingness to experiment,
acceptance of new ideas, and fascination with technology
reflected American attitudes and tastes. In later years, a mane
of white hair, an ever-present black cigar, and white suits
made him stand out in any crowd. Like his own Connecticut
yankee, he might have said: 'For I never care to do a thing
in a quiet way; it's got to be theatrical or I don't take any
interest in it'.[5] His books summoned up a rich frontier past

woven from freedom and variety that was vivid in the imaginations if not always in the actual experience of many readers.

Mark Twain began his career as a western humorist, and was popular as a lecturer and national cultural figure rather than as a novelist. His *bon mots* entered common parlance, and often revealed outrage at inequity and snobbery. He employed wit to highlight the human condition, to praise goodness, and to knock expensive hats off humbugs. In reviewing *Innocents Abroad*, Howells noted this quality: '. . . we do not remember where [humor] is indulged in at the cost of the weak or the helpless, or where it is insolent, with all its sauciness and irreverence.'[6]

Mark Twain belonged to no school and espoused no literary theory, but he was a Realist. His characters became allegorical by representing national attitudes and future hopes. He did not always relish the limited role of humorist, and Howells saw in him 'a nature whose tragical seriousness broke in the laughter which the unwise took for the whole of him'.[7] His vacillation between reform and art reflected a conflict between the need for worldly success and contempt for social attitudes that ignored individual freedom. The inability to embrace a unifying esthetic flawed his work. Critics wondered how the same man could write the evocative *Life on the Mississippi* (1883), and the contrived, lifeless *Personal Recollections of Joan of Arc* (1896). But Howells once again saw the clue: 'At heart Clemens was romantic, and he would have the world of fiction stately and handsome and whatever the real world was not; but he was not romanticistic, and he was too helplessly an artist not to wish his own work to show life as he had seen it'.[8]

The public knew little of Mark Twain's brooding last years, when the death of his wife and daughter called life's meaning into question. For millions of Americans, his presence and writings recalled a recognizable past amid change. He used a deflating wit to praise variety and tolerance. And in turning inward to examine his own origins and motives, he illustrated an increasing tendency among artists to explain the external world with internal evidence.

Howells, Mark Twain, and other Realists caught the tone and quality of ongoing change that permeated life. They delineated many predicaments that alternately gratified and bewildered real people. Orville Dryfoos, one-time farmer and new oil tycoon in *A Hazard of New Fortunes*, voiced a personal response to industrialism. Yesterday would not come again, and tomorrow was unpredictable. His family could not gain solace by rejecting the system that had suddenly gratified their wishes:

> There's no farm any more to go back to. The fields is full of gas-wells and oil-wells and hell-holes generally . . . . If I was to give all I'm worth, we couldn't go back to the farm any more than them girls in there could go back and be little children.[9]

Developing national unity provoked fresh interest in regional 'local color'. Mark Twain and Bret Harte spoke for the West, and George W. Cable's works displayed southern qualities. Sarah Orne Jewett's brilliant stories in *The Country of the Pointed Firs* (1896) depicted 'a New England gone to seed, a race dying out in old maids, eccentric men and deserted farm houses', as young people left the countryside.[10] Other writers tried to focus the receding images of the Great Border and the Old Northwest.

Hamlin Garland typified distrust of the nationalism and centralized power that threatened unique regional qualities. Born in Wisconsin in 1860, he suffered the rigors of farm work on the harsh Dakota plains. He celebrated pioneer virtues, but attacked the sentimental agrarian myth in *Main Traveled Roads* (1891). In the manifesto *Crumbling Idols* (1894), Garland offered a counterpoint to Howellsian Realism, arguing that 'the similarities do not please, do not forever stimulate as do the differences'. He alternately disliked the sophisticated East and longed to share its cultural authority. Skeptical of tastes derived from Old World culture, he praised democracy and individualism. 'The West should aim to be wise rather than cultured. Wisdom is democratic, culture is aristocratic. Wisdom is knowledge of principle, culture is knowledge of forms and accepted conventions. . .'.[11] Local color would help unify Americans by celebrating their diverse qualities in a shrinking world community.

Garland's naive earnestness fairly invited the charge of provincialism. Henry Blake Fuller, a student of the new urban frontier, parodied local color in an amusing novella, 'The Downfall of Abner Joyce', modeled on Garland's career. 'It was their cardinal tenet that a report on an aspect of nature was a work of art . . .' he noted wryly in discussing the regionalists' dislike of sophistication and analysis.[12]

The vigorous local color movement of the 1890s testified to fears of cultural uniformity and industrial power. It was active in every industrializing nation, but could not arrest the trend toward world styles. Character analysis and the individual's relation to others and to social rules triumphed in fiction, as Henry James's career proved. James's early works dealt with the American scene, which he left in 1875 for England. His studies of individual confrontations with symbolic social manners, and of the challenge of American vigor to European stability, made him a world figure. Though he appreciated Old World order, James never abandoned his American heritage. His realism differed from Howells', but served the same general purpose. In depicting the subtle impacts of old values on new personalities, he delineated much of his country's movement toward nationhood and world culture.

Realism in all its varieties triumphed, but like all doctrines it became a formula, and faced challenges from younger writers in the 1890s. Howells avoided overt sexuality and determinism, and doubted that Naturalism fitted the optimistic and expansive American experience. Zola would do for France, but America had avoided most of the excesses he described. For Howells, Naturalism explained life only with a dogmatic universalism that ignored unique qualities.

The young Frank Norris disagreed, however much he appreciated Howells's encouragement. Norris thought the Realists were tepid and parochial in emphasizing Howells's 'smiling aspects of life' while ignoring individual and social brutality. The good novel had 'the wide world for a range, and the unplumbed depths of the human heart, and the black, unsearched penetralia of the soul of man'. Though his charges against Howells were unfair, Norris's brand of Naturalism attracted young authors who wanted writing that 'draws conclusions from a whole congeries of forces, social tendencies, race impulses, [and] devotes itself not to a study of men, but of man'.[13]

American naturalists actually relied less on continental theories than on romanticized naturalistic devices. Norris's *McTeague* (1899) depicted the atavism of a San Francisco dentist at the mercy of fate, but who also was simply unable to manage complex new social demands. *The Octopus* (1901), and *The Pit* (1903) used the growth and distribution of wheat to symbolize awesome, impersonal natural forces that controlled mankind. With less melodrama, Stephen Crane examined the individual in an indifferent world in *The Red Badge of Courage* (1895) and in several distinguished short stories. But Theodore Dreiser came closest to formal Naturalism in *Sister Carrie*, finished in 1900 but not issued until 1912. His use of an ongoing sense of endless time, and rich details of daily life made the book hard reading. But in depicting the encounter of rural inexperience with urban complexity, poverty with affluence, personal ambition with collective indifference, Dreiser captured the tone of America's passage into the modern world.

The same desire to retain American qualities and concern for substantive realism motivated creative talents in the 'fine' arts of music and painting. Although America's musical heritage was weak, musicians also felt the mutual attractions of growing national identity and cosmopolitanism. The flowering of Romanticism coincided with the improved travel and communication that brought both musical news and talent to the New World. Newspaper critics avidly discussed the latest operas and symphonies and evaluated distinguished soloists. Easy transportation, improved facilities, and new advertising methods allowed many cities and towns to host musical figures. The fine arts were a basic urban attraction to youths leaving the countryside.

The expanding middle class supported both performances and training. Mass produced instruments, especially the piano, and inexpensive scores fed a boom in musical education. Many American students returning from European study taught in new musical institutions. The Oberlin Conservatory opened in 1865, and there were prestigious schools in Cincinnati, Chicago, Boston, and Baltimore. Between 1865 and 1900, wealthy patrons and community organizations established concert halls in every important eastern and midwestern city.

Europe's musical dominance was most obvious in opera, whose aristocratic qualities and unreality countered American concern for democracy and realism. But Americans had a traditional love of the theater and operetta. The works of Johann Strauss and Jacques Offenbach captivated audiences, who also applauded the satire of Gilbert and Sullivan. 'Light opera' seemed unpretentious yet beautiful, escapist but somehow concerned with people.

Grand opera did not languish, and Americans saw a formidable array of celebrities. New York's lavish Metropolitan Opera established the repertoire and had no serious rivals until later challenges from Chicago and San Francisco. Audiences liked Donizetti, Bellini, and Verdi, but Wagner's spectacular works provoked intense discussion about the direction of music.

Nearly every town boasted an opera house, but production costs restricted opera to a few wealthy cities. Local theaters served a visiting celebrity more often than a full production. America produced a few outstanding vocalists, but no significant composer of operas. But those who heard

Nellie Melba, Ernestine Schumann-Heink, Enrico Caruso, and the de Reszke brothers agreed with a critic's pardonable hyperbole: 'Fortunate public, destined to be the envy of future generations'.[14]

The symphony orchestra vied with operatic companies as a mark of civic culture. Boston wished to offset New York's growing cultural power by emphasizing the arts. Chicago announced her arrival as the West's chief city with musical and artistic institutions. San Francisco was clearly the dominant city in the Far West, and every major regional center wanted cultural symbols.

This competition illustrated regional tensions, but rested on a genuine interest in the arts. Didactic observers praised the 'elevating' tendencies of music and painting. 'If such performances of both sacred and secular music were more frequent, we should have less drunkenness, less wife-beating, less spending of winter gains, less winter pauperism', a reviewer noted.[15] Nationalism played a large part in establishing cultural bases. Americans hoped to replace Europe in the arts, just as they wanted to supersede her in industrial growth and political freedom. Increasing wealth and security also prompted civic leaders to look beyond profit. 'Many of them understood that life held finer things than successful businesses', an artist noted of Chicago's leaders, 'and they tried to make such things actual. They supported schools, museums, universities, opera and orchestras'.[16]

In the decades after Appomattox, every large city established or refurbished its symphony society. Major orchestras developed in Boston, Philadelphia, and New York, and groups in Chicago, Cleveland, and western cities testified to interest in music outside the monied East. Conductors like Theodore Thomas and Leopold Damrosch of New York disciplined their orchestras and developed public support. Thomas's tours became famous, and he stubbornly taught audiences both 'classical' and 'Romantic' music.

Foreign conductors, performers, and composers took

advantage of the American market. Anton Dvořák directed
the American Conservatory in New York from 1892 to 1895,
and first performed his 'New World Symphony' in 1893.
Tchaikovsky visited in 1891 to premier his second piano
concerto. Saint-Saëns toured briefly in 1906 and again in
1915. And Gustav Mahler conducted for the Metropolitan
Opera, then for the New York Philharmonic between 1907
and 1911.

Audiences heard a full range of European music.
Beethoven and Mozart dominated programs, though
America did not escape the furious debate between the
partisans of Brahms and Wagner. Audiences generally liked
Romantic music, some of which quickly disappeared, and
were unreceptive to innovators or 'moderns' like Richard
Strauss.

Composers fared worse than performers. Lacking a
serious national heritage, they could either innovate and
alienate audiences, or write derivative works that could not
compete with European music. And in a medium requiring
capital for performance, the composer became subordinate
to the conductor who chose programs. Both had to accept
audience taste or risk an uncertain educational process. The
cerebral nature of formal music also inhibited its general
appeal, especially in view of popular attachment to folk
melody and the 'light classics'. Patrons could not study
music in a museum, like a painting; or buy a copy for their
home, like a book. Most musical events gained newspaper
coverage for news content rather than esthetics, and poor
criticism hurt both composers and performers. And composers received less public assistance than sculptors or mural
painters.

A prestigious 'New England Group' composed a modified
Romantic music, but most commentators seemed interested
chiefly in developing a national style within the Romantic
tradition. Chopin wrote for Poland; Smetana and Dvořák
for Bohemia. A school celebrated Russia's qualities; and a
Frenchman, George Bizet, wrote the best Spanish opera,

'Carmen'. Nationalistic composers everywhere hoped to retain local color and individualism within world culture.

The 'New World Symphony' prompted discussion of a distinctive American idiom, but attention turned to Edward MacDowell (1861–1908) rather than Dvořák. MacDowell developed a rather quiet Romanticism after studying in Germany. He hoped to reflect the American temper, but saw that local color was not enough. 'I do not believe in "lifting" a Navaho theme and furbishing it into some kind of musical composition and calling it American music', he told Hamlin Garland. 'Our problem is not so simple as that.' He sought a tone rather than a form. 'What we must arrive at is the youthful optimistic vitality and the undaunted tenacity of spirit that characterizes the American man.'[17]

MacDowell was Romantic in seeing music as 'a language of the intangible, a kind of soul-language' that enriched individual lives and provided universality above cultural differences.[18] His broad second piano concerto was popular; but the short, impressionistic songs and piano pieces best fulfilled his esthetic ideals. A mystical belief in nature's basic harmony and spaciousness combined with folk rhythms to establish the 'American' qualities of MacDowell's music.

The expense of performing music, its cerebral nature, and a familiar European repertoire all inhibited national musical style. But painting rested on a stronger tradition and commanded more talent. The early struggle for identity made painters defensive, but they had won a place in national life by mid-century. An expanding middle class bought paintings; easier travel broadened general taste, and allowed students to sample contrasting styles. Artists congregated in cities for companionship and inspiration. Newspapers, books, and magazines offered a wealth of ideas and helped bring the United States into the exciting, if often arcane, mainstream of international art.

American painters had studied abroad before and a few had even established careers in England and Italy. But post-war students felt like pioneers, and were imbued with a sense of revolutionary creative change. Alienation from American life motivated them less than an earnest desire for good training and individual development.

In the 1860s and 1870s, many students went to Germany, which resembled the United States in her movement toward national unity. The 'Düsseldorf School' commanded brief attention for stylized historical scenes and meticulous landscapes. Emanuel Leutze's 'Washington Crossing the Delaware' typified the school's concern for elegant finish that revealed little trace of the painter. The Düsseldorf artists attempted to combine academic principles and familiar events in a respectable pseudo-realism. But their meticulous drawing, hard finish, and primary colors made even the most heroic subject lifeless. 'The Düsseldorf school always strikes *twelve*', a critic complained. 'You see the brush and the palette. You do not see the mind, the soul of the painter'.[19] Eastman Johnson was among the few outstanding Americans who studied at Düsseldorf, and used his training in rural *genre* scenes and realistic portraits.

American painters wavered between the desire to master a certified formal manner, and to express their individuality, and the genial city of Munich provided a haven for those who disliked rigid standards. The Munich painters avoided hard colors, the dominant outline, and heroic subjects. Their thick brush-work and blended colors made the sumptuous 'brown sauce of Munich' appealing. Their subject-matter, such as the American Frank Duveneck's Turkish page-boy sprawled amid a litter of highly paintable exotic objects, pleased those concerned to delight the eye rather than the memory. Though practitioners of the style often sacrificed subject-matter for dashing brushwork, Munich paintings radiated a calm unity with rich color and texture, and dealt with reality.

Paris remained the capital of academicism, since France alone had a central system for training artists in the various branches of the *École des Beaux-Arts*. A historic gallic love of formal elegance, and conservative government patronage produced a system of education that emphasized line drawing and conventional subject-matter. Classroom teaching rested on the idea of transferring discipline. As the Irish novelist George Moore recalled: 'the world in the fields and in the streets, that living world full of passionate color and joyous movement, was but an illusive temptation; the studio model was the truth, the truth in essence; if we could draw the nude, we could draw anything'.[20] The practice did not always match the theory. 'They are taught the beautiful as one teaches algebra', complained Eugène Delacroix.[21] Most training that emphasized the formal line produced only what Henry James called 'the conscientious nude'.[22]

But Americans needed both sound training and a congenial atmosphere in which to explore European art, and academic study did not stultify much genuine talent. *La vie bohème* shocked some American students, but neither painter nor poet had to justify his calling in a Paris whose artistic atmosphere was 'as thick as mud', according to the young Robert Henri.[23]

The French capital was also a base camp for forays into neighboring countries, and while students complained about traditional canons, they learned a great deal from first-hand viewing in Europe's galleries. Americans especially appreciated the rich color and character in Dutch and Flemish works. 'The Dutch are my ideal', wrote the budding impressionist J. Alden Weir. 'They are a very sincere and conscientious people; it makes one feel the shallowness of the French.'[24]

The Spaniards also influenced many Americans. The Spanish master Velasquez combined rich surface qualities of personal expression with evocative interpretation. In seeking the impression of a whole personality, he had avoided fine drawing and petty details. His broad brushstrokes created an exciting sense of motion, but muted colors and careful lighting produced a subtle harmony. 'In his grave and lofty symphony of black and white and gray, Velasquez suppressed the negligible . . .' the American painter Edwin H. Blashfield said.[25]

Students were impatient of formal study, and disliked academic rules, but Americans profited from discipline and exposure to art. They ranged freely over the past for examples and the best studied old masters without copying them. Common sense and sober analysis drew them to vital sources like the Dutch and Spaniards. Skeptical of formulas, Americans retained a strong preference for realism and character over elegance.

Students returning home complained of public indifference, yet they were more secure than any predecessors. The arts never commanded a mass audience, but prosperity and urbanization generated both interest in and facilities for the arts. Shows, galleries, new teaching institutions, and critical attention revealed concern for painting. Americans also exhibited at the world fairs of 1867, 1873, 1889, and 1900, and dominated those at home of 1876, 1893, and 1901.

Every large city had a bohemian section, but New York became the mecca for aspiring poets, sculptors, and painters. It was close to Europe, and an *entrepôt* for both ideas and goods, was the national publishing center, and the biggest market for art work. Its impersonality offered artists a kind of security and freedom, and the city was an endless source of subject-matter. 'I determined to come to New York, sink or swim, survive or perish, rather than rot in the miserable mediocrity of a western studio', Carroll Beckwith of Chicago said, after studying with Carolus-Duran in Paris.[26]

Few artists lived well, but many worked as illustrators and engravers in the expanding publishing industry. 'Yes, we return from Europe, undecided whether we'll go back to Paris for the rest of our life, or stay here and build a studio big enough for our work', Will Low recalled, 'and then, after a while, we're blamed glad to make drawings for some magazine at thirty dollars per drawing'.[27] A few men such as Edwin Austen Abbey attained international stature as illustrators. The *art nouveau* and handcraft artists created magazine covers, posters, and prints, with rich colors and sensual lines. Craftsmanship and public demand for quality production made engraving and lithography important art forms.

Artists who were not engravers or could not sell their works usually taught in one of the museums, academies, or private schools that met new demands for esthetic progress. A few famous painters like William Merritt Chase became noted teachers, with lucrative city studios and country workshops. But other frustrated artists could only agree that 'whereas it is very difficult for an artist to make his living by practicing his trade, it is quite easy for him to make a living teaching others to practice it'.[28]

William Morris Hunt decried academic teaching methods and urged pupils to avoid critics and books in favor of observation and development of individual tastes. Holding that Columbus would never have discovered America if he had heard a lecture about it, Hunt snapped: 'I have known a deaf painter, but not a blind one.'[29] Hunt dominated the Boston art world in the 1870s, and taught hundreds of students by force of example. Few other cities boasted a painter with his quick tongue, but many had public and private art teaching facilities.

Schools were one aspect of efforts to focus attention on the arts, and to raise the standards of training and taste. Many artists regretted the lack of official support, except through occasional public works, but lack of governmental aid was a blessing in disguise. A representative system would have enthroned local color or derivative classicism. The annual shows and awards of the private National Academy of Design represented success in the absence of official patronage, and the Academy's prestigious directors and fellows were a national jury.

The institution developed strong ties to Europe in its efforts to integrate American and world culture. The Academy and comparable organizations outside New York were conservative, yet no single standard ever dominated national art. Prescribed taste reigned but did not rule. The interested public read of world events, and saw a cross-section of painting at the new museums. The Society of American Artists, the Society of Painters in Pastel, the New York Etching Club, the American Watercolor Society, and regional groups complemented academic tastes and illustrated artistic variety. Some kind of academic standard was inevitable, and in America it was less restrictive than governmental or royal institutions.

The new museums rising in major cities complemented the Academy's search for order and satisfied the public's desire to see art. The same themes of uplift and esthetic development that motivated many painters ran through museum charters. Founders hoped to improve the public with the 'finer' things of life. 'There is no education like intelligent seeing', one spokesman noted.[30]

Whatever the merits of the theories that prompted their founders, museums illustrated a general desire to move beyond materialism. They were usually privately endowed, but often obtained some public support. The rich and socially prominent naturally headed fund drives, and their work produced impressive results. By 1876, the Boston Museum of Fine Arts, the Metropolitan Museum of New York, and the Philadelphia Art Museum were major institutions. In the next decade, Chicago, St. Louis, Cincinnati, and Detroit opened museums. Brooklyn and Pittsburgh followed in the 1890s, while Harvard, Bowdoin, and other colleges established important galleries with private bequests.

The desire for expertise and orderly growth entered museum work. Curators moved away from the cluttered hanging style common to European institutions in favor of special lighting and individual arrangements to emphasize both old and new masters. In time, separate rooms housed unique collections under expert care. Publication departments supported scholarly research and issued pamphlets, bulletins, and prints. Like academies, museums had to accept reigning taste, though most acquired works of living Americans, and were generally ahead of the public.

Dealers served both institutional and private buyers. Individualistic artists disliked gallery owners' affection for 'safe' old masters and European academicians. But contemporary American and Continental works entered a widening stream of purchases. By 1880 there were an estimated 150 notable private collections in the United States. 'At one time, in the Eighties, wealthy New Yorkers were really forced to have a gallery', an observer recalled, if only to protect themselves against the charge of materialism.[31]

Private collectors usually relied on dealers to choose good paintings that were also sound investments. This was more risky than selecting stocks and bonds. Today's hero was likely to be tomorrow's footnote in a history book, while the unknown might become immortal. The turbulence of artistic reputations restrained purchasers, who inevitably preferred Donatello to Monet or unknown Americans.

But every rich man's taste was not a desert. W. W. Corcoran left the nation a fabulous collection. Charles Lang Freer also gave an impressive array of ancient porcelain and china, oriental art, and Whistleriana to the nation. Henry Clay Frick gathered old masters, and J. P. Morgan amassed rare books, manuscripts, and *objets*. Mr and Mrs Henry O. Havemeyer bequeathed both old and modern paintings to the Metropolitan Museum. Many other patrons gave money and art objects to public institutions, and commissioned knowledgeable painters to locate important works abroad. Mary Cassatt and J. Alden Weir secured paintings by El Greco, Corot, Courbet, Manet, and many Impressionists for collectors and institutions.

The publishing revolution supported special columnists dealing with art, culture, and popular taste. Most local newsmen were interested in personalities and unusual events, but the *Nation*, *Harper's*, art journals, and major newspapers employed professional reviewers. They joined with new college professors to build at least the foundations for studies in art history and criticism. The interest of these men and the people they served indicated concern for the direction of art, and a desire for lasting values. A few critics understood that their discipline was beginning to reflect personal rather than formulistic tastes, just as painting revealed a steadily growing trend to individual expression. 'Criticism is therefore no longer dogmatic, but analytical and appreciative', one wrote in 1892, '[and] it seeks to understand a painter's temperament and to see his work from his own point of view; it may have preferences, but those preferences derive their value only from the personality of the critic who expresses them'.[32] Esthetic tolerance did not enter every viewer, convulsed before a 'barbaric' Monet, or enthralled by an Abbott Thayer angel. But like other changes in art expression and public taste, tolerance was part of accepting esthetics based on change rather than tradition.

The subject-matter and styles of painting revealed both a growing concern for the new, and a desire for comforting familiarity. The general public did not understand or see the array of work available to the interested few near museums or art colonies. But people bought millions of lithographs and prints depicting familiar or desirable qualities of American life. Genre remained popular, even as artists sought symbolism or individuality. Eastman Johnson gained a strong reputation for romanticized but highly professional scenes of rural life. A major part of Winslow Homer's work depicted country life and the mystery of the sea to an increasingly urbanized population. A few artists offered exotic city-scapes; John Weir and Thomas Anschutz painted somewhat romanticized but noteworthy views of industrial production and labor.

But most genre painting was literary or anecdotal, in what an acid critic called 'the Kiss Mummy' style.[33] A host of canine and feline friends romped with idealized children or mourned at the coffins of dead masters. Radiating human qualities, they were 'clamoring to teach you that, if you are but little lower than the angels, dogs are but little lower than you'.[34] Scenes of harmonious countrysides and blissful romance appealed to urban buyers who missed fancied rural contentment. The same mannerism convinced others of the wisdom of avoiding industrial cities. Yet a great deal of genre painting was vital and realistic, especially in the magazines, books, and advertising that entered millions of homes.

Earlier painters had established an equally important tradition in portraiture. Gilbert Stuart and John Singleton Copley attained international recognition, and their studies of George Washington and other leading Americans had entered the national consciousness. Artists' desires to prove their country's claims to individualism, truth and freedom had produced realistic portraiture. Much early work had reflected both a painful search for literal truth, however unflattering, and a simple lack of training. A defensive belief that honesty was better than glamor in portraiture reinforced a desire to depict character without bravura technique.

Many artists lived well from portrait commissions, which attested to both rising prosperity and concern for painting. Although photography and contact with the plush European tradition undermined portraiture as a means of livelihood for painters, concern for character in portraiture was hardly dead in 1865, as the work of Thomas Eakins of Philadelphia well proved. Study with Gérôme in Paris reinforced his commitment to an interpretive realism that rested on solid workmanship and avoided salon frills. The bluff, moody Eakins taught at the Pennsylvania Academy until he resigned in 1886 after a controversy over using nude male models in mixed classes. His crusty manner and insistence on detailed study of anatomy alternately frightened and inspired devoted students. He taught them to study the human musculature and skeleton in minute detail to develop a sense of balance and proportion. Pupils even dissected corpses and studied still photographs of models in motion.

'Get the character of things', he said. 'I hate this average kind of work.'[35]

Eakins's paintings of active men illustrated his teaching. Wrestlers, oarsmen, hunters, and fishermen peopled his larger canvases. His most famous work, 'The Gross Clinic' of 1875 scandalized polite Philadelphia by showing an operation, complete with exposed incision and a horrified onlooker. Doctor Gross, the magisterial central figure, stood poised in light, exhuding a sense of command and courage, the symbol of Eakins' belief in individual quality.

Despite the controversy over his teaching methods, Eakins retained a clientele. His keen eye for outer details also saw inner traits, and the portraits revealed a fine grasp of personal psychology. 'He saw what distinguishes anyone from a distance', a contemporary noted, 'before the features come into play'.[36] He was masterful at catching a single evocative moment or gesture with universal application, and Eakins endowed varied subjects with contemplative gravity and symbolism. His realism was in the American grain. So was the chilly loneliness he gave the oarsmen, prizefighters, doctors, and concert singers seeking to master both a medium and themselves. He was often idealistic in seeking allegory, but Eakins' best pictures radiated an austere mystery suspended in time, yet personally comprehensible to viewers.

Eakins owed much to the examples of Rembrandt, Hals, and Velasquez. His dark palette, shaded light, and details were all comfortably 'old masterish', rich yet dignified. But a distinct sense of time and place marked the American origins of his works.

Yet for all his power, Eakins offered no point of departure for an *avant garde*, and more cosmopolitan men initiated a movement that paralleled his realism. Frank Duveneck returned from Munich to pursue an impressive career as a portraitist and teacher. 'Duveneck's Boys' broke down formal planes, lines, and volumes. They sought instead a vivid and often momentary impression, conveyed in broad, thick

brushstrokes that blended at the edges, and with light
suffused over the canvas. Munich's 'brown sauce' gave way
to higher colors, and a growing concern for light.

Duveneck's friend William Merritt Chase typified the
bravura manner. 'A Beau Brummel with the vitality of ten
men . . .', the elegant Chase painted steadily, and taught
students in a lavish New York studio, on European tours,
and at a retreat in Massachusetts.[37] He took pride in a rich
manner that produced shimmering highlights and motion,
and he painted brass and other surfaces that reflected
colored light. His still-lifes of fish and fruit were almost
standard fixtures in well-to-do parlors. Chase produced a
sumptuous, appealing canvas, and his rapid brushwork
became legendary. 'Take plenty of time for your picture',
he allegedly told a landscape class, 'take two hours if you
need it'.[38]

Chase influenced youthful painters who saw in his
personal dash and fluid style a delightful alternative to both
academicism and didactic realism. Critics called him 'the
ablest painter of face values that America has yet produced'.[39] The charge was somewhat unfair. Chase was
seldom reflective and disliked art criticism, but he studied
painting closely as an inveterate gallery-goer. He sought
spontaneity, and emotionally accepted Whistler's doctrine
that a good painting was self-sufficient, an object of intrinsic
beauty as well as a source for reflection. Chase thought that
a canvas should display 'truth, interesting treatment, and
quality'. Truth was 'the impression of a thing well seen'.
Treatment involved 'the interest of the artist . . .'. And
quality was 'a perfect balance of all the parts [that] may be
manifested in color or line or composition'.[40]

The growing concern for elegant composition and suave
treatment was part of the urge for cosmopolitan connec-
tions, and reflected a fear that domestic painting was backward. Both artists and patrons wanted wider expression and
refinement than had characterized earlier American art.
Painters of the 1870s rejected the solemn moralism that

1. Frank Duveneck, 'Italian Girl'. *Courtesy*, Los Angeles County Museum of Art. Bequest of Mary D. Tyler.

2. Thomas Eakins, 'Dr John H. Brinton'. *Courtesy*, National Gallery of Art, Washington D.C. Lent by the Medical Museum of the Armed Forces Institute of Pathology.

3. John Singer Sargent, 'Mrs William Crowninshield Endicott'. *Courtesy*, National Gallery of Art, Washington D.C. Gift of Louise Thoron Endicott in memory of Mr and Mrs William Crowninshield Endicott.

4. John White Alexander, American, 1856–1915, 'Isabella and the Pot of Basil'. Oil on Canvas, $75\frac{1}{2} \times 35\frac{3}{4}$ in. Signed and dated lower left: John Alexander, '97. *Courtesy*, Museum of Fine Arts, Boston. Gift of Ernest Wadsworth Longfellow.

5. William Merritt Chase, 'Onions'. *Courtesy*, Los Angeles County Museum of Art. Bequest of Mary D. Keeler.

6. William Merritt Chase, 'The Open Air Breakfast'. *Courtesy*, Toledo, Ohio. Gift of Florence Scott Libbey.

7. William Morris Hunt, 'Study of a Female Head'. Charcoal drawing. *Courtesy,* Bowdoin College Museum of Art, Brunswick, Maine.

8. Winslow Homer, 'The Incoming Tide', Watercolor. *Courtesy*, Collection of the American Academy of Arts and Letters.

9. John Singer Sargent, 'Lake O'Hara'. *Courtesy*, Fogg Art Museum, Harvard University. Gift of Edward W. Forbes.

10. Maurice
Prendergast, 'Central
Park 1900'. Water-
color, 14 × 21¾ in.
Courtesy, Collection of
the Whitney Museum
of American Art, New
York.

11. Theodore
Robinson, 'Woman
Sewing, Giverny'.
Courtesy, The Roland
P. Murdock
Collection,
Wichita, Kansas.

12. John H. Twachtman, 'Drying Sails'. *Courtesy*, of the Smithsonian Institution, Freer Gallery of Art, Washington, D.C.

13. J. Alden Weir, 'Building a Dam, Shetucket'. *Courtesy*, Cleveland Museum of Art. Purchase from the J. H. Wade Fund.

14. Edwin H. Blashfield, 'Oil Sketch of Mural for the Iowa State Capitol Building'. *Courtesy*, Des Moines Art Center. Gift of Robert Brady.

15. William Morris Hunt, American, 1824–1879, 'Anahita. The Flight of Night'. Oil on Canvas, 62 × 99 in. Painted in 1878. *Courtesy*, Museum of Fine Arts, Boston. Gift of H. N. Slater, Mrs E. Slater Kerrigan, and Mrs R. Slater Murphy, in memory of their mother, Mabel Hunt Slater.

16. Kenyon Cox, 'The Arts'. Mural Decoration. *Courtesy*, Library of Congress.

dominated both painting and criticism. Tired of the historic search for grandeur and uplift, they wanted art to instruct and please within esthetic guidelines. Chase's work and influential teaching showed both the steady erosion of literalism and the appeals of painterly expression. And his paintings had many intrinsic merits. The best portraits were exciting personality studies. His salon pieces offered depth and integrity of design, and the landscapes were delightful. His vigor was an important tonic for American art.

The most glamorous American painter lived in England. Born in Italy of wealthy American parents, John Singer Sargent remained something of a prodigy until his death in 1925. His social success and international style made him a *beau idéal* for many aspiring painters. Sargent studied with the tolerant and progressive Carolus-Duran in Paris. He did not visit the United States until 1876, then lived in London, travelling frequently on the Continent and across the Atlantic. In time, he became a member of the Royal Academy, and even declined a knighthood from Edward VII, while firmly retaining American citizenship.

His ability to capture dazzling effects, and the use of blended color for more than its own sake marked Sargent for a somewhat ambivalent success. 'He was one of those fortunate men who at the very threshold of his career had apparently nothing more to learn.'[41] He produced a great volume of works in several mediums and styles, which seemed to prove the complaint that he was merely facile. Critics admired 'the dash, the spontaneity, the sparkling life of the painter's handling . . .' but professed to miss depth.[42] Somewhat like Whistler, he gave the impression of working hastily. 'He was doing his judge's gown [for a portrait] today', an amazed young observer recalled after watching him paint, 'and he dashed right ahead as though he were painting a fence until he finished it, and he never made a mistake once!'[43] But he actually painted with great care, and unless a subject eluded him, released no work which further attention might improve.

Sargent shocked the Paris art world of 1884 with a striking portrait of 'Madame Gautreau' in colors and a pose said
not to exist in nature. His salon picture 'El Jaleo', depicting
a Spanish dancer swirling to the tambourines in a vignette of
motion and life, was impressive. The celebrated 'Daughters
of Edward D. Boit', showing four children of a wealthy
family, revealed brushwork, light, and integrated design
that merited comparison with older masters.

His *portraits d'apparat* of subjects in unguarded but characteristic moments were most famous. He caught Robert
Louis Stevenson slightly off the canvas center, leaning
anxiously on long legs, full of nervous energy and apprehension. A portrait of Theodore Roosevelt was less successful for being more studied, yet it revealed the President's
energy and toughness. Pundits said with a variety of mean-
ings about both men that Sargent's portrait of Chase was
'more like Chase than Chase himself'.[44]

Sargent became an international celebrity, producing
studies of the rich and famous, caught in fashionable clothes
amid elegant decor, in which he blended color and light
without detracting from the subject. He also painted
numerous group portraits of academic, professional, and
social figures, and devoted several years to impressive murals
in the Boston Public Library.

Sargent's huge output was inevitably uneven. Variations
of quality reflected inner anxieties, for despite fame and
fortune, he remained personally insecure. Though more
perceptive than Chase or Duveneck, he shared their love of
display and the contradictory need for subtle interpretation
often just slightly out of reach. Yet he was an important
realist, developing a conception of art and life that emphasized motion and change. He used daring color combinations
and designs, and built up effects with carefully blended
brushstrokes that diminished formal lines without losing
volume. His watercolors displayed an evocative sense of
detachment and solitude firmly in the traditional American
concern for man's relation to natural order. Sargent typified

the continuing need of American artists to define enveloping space, motion, and individual character, while meeting the challenges and temptations of academic elegance. He inspired many others to test new artistic problems, and his own work enriched world painting with interpreted reality.

Earlier American painters had sought a viable 'history' style that might gain the respectability of antique associations and allegory for the new Republic. But even the best works of John Vanderlyn, Washington Allston, and Thomas Cole were monumental rather than moving or instructive. At the middle of the century, the landscape dominated painting, and in subtle ways met the need for both symbolism and self-expression. The natural landscape was familiar and 'real' to individuals, yet symbolized mankind's relation to a universal order. It was predictable and thus reassuring, but was varied enough for individual interpretation. And while nature appealed to emotions, it was not artificial or decadent like man-made arts.

Some landscapists worked with meticulous detail, while others sought an Emersonian allegory in nature. Frederic Church depicted a mystical, awesome world born more of inner yearnings toward infinity and release than of observation. Albert Bierstadt romanticized mountains, rivers, and canyons into a dramatic 'history' painting. And George Inness moved steadily to a muted, poetic style built on reflection and impressions drawn from both memory and observation.

Europeans also sought a landscape style that united nature and man. Corot's harmony, familiar subject-matter, and warm coloration impressed many Americans. 'He knows the worth of mystery and of hiding the appearance of hard work', William Morris Hunt insisted.[45]

The small group of painters who worked in the forests outside Paris also influenced Americans. The 'Barbizon School' employed a warm, blended manner that evoked impressions from both the eye and memory. They rejected classical symbols in favor of peasants and the countryside, which was heresy enough to those who insisted that art pertained only to 'dignified' subjects. The Barbizon painters sketched outdoors, but relied on studio finishing to produce interpreted recollection. They were not concerned with a new treatment of light, but were important in the search for a broadened realism.

The Barbizon painters became popular in the United States for several reasons. They glorified rural verities amid urbanization and industrialization. Their human figures worked in familiar natural settings, and became non-classical allegories. Americans accepted the 'common' subjects that repelled Europeans because painters like Jean François Millet 'did not paint peasants as they really looked but idealized them as symbolic figures'.[46] And the warm, blended colors appealed to the eye and senses. Prints and photographs of 'The Gleaners' and 'The Sower' hung in many parlors and studios. 'The Man With the Hoe' prompted Edwin Markham to write one of the most popular of American poems.

The nervous, energetic William Morris Hunt bought Millet's paintings, and championed 'modern' French art in Boston. He allowed students to break down conventional line. 'Can you see an egg against a white background?' he asked, 'Not by drawing a line around it can you make it evident!' Hunt rejected both the academic manner and intent. 'You are to draw *not reality, but the appearance of reality!*'[47] The precise line was not the truth; mere elegance was not beauty. Creative art relied on bonds of recollection and interpretation between artist and viewer.

By the 1870s, 'Impressionism' was more than the *succès de scandale* that shocked Paris at the 'Salon des Refusés' in 1863. American painters living in Europe were familiar with the style. Sargent helped secure government purchase of Manet's 'Olympia' in 1889, and Mary Cassatt advised collectors to buy the new paintings. The public got its first significant glimpse of Impressionist works in 1886, when the Paris dealer Durand-Ruel exhibited some 300 canvases in New York. The art public displayed interest, puzzlement, and some outrage, but the general reaction was more tolerant than in France. Durand-Ruel claimed that the sale of some $18,000 worth of pictures rescued Monet and Renoir from poverty, and that the American reaction enhanced Impressionism's general appeal.[48]

When Impressionist painting first appeared, the works of Courbet, Corot, and the Barbizon painters already seemed slightly old-fashioned, touched with sentiment and elegy. George Inness in particular, and landscape treatment in general, had moved steadily toward the blurred edge and light colors. But Americans had not embraced the Impressionists' use of high colors in short strokes which the eye blended optically at a distance from the canvas. They were still more concerned with the ways light illuminated objects, than with it as a separate factor of sense or nature.

Americans accepted Impressionism as a legitimate experiment against conventionality, but were uncertain about its esthetic canons. The sensuous appeals of pure color and light seemed insubstantial and deceptive to people concerned with observable reality and personal qualities. Impressionism's bright colors, one result of a revolution in chemical and tubed paints, seemed raw and unfinished to those critics seeking subtle harmony.[49]

Many Americans praised Degas' skillful drawing and perspective, and approved Renoir's charm. But they initially disliked the Impressionists' concern for 'the fugitive aspect of things . . .' typified in the everchanging, and therefore disturbing, play of light, or the vanishing and uncharacteristic expression on a subject's face.[50] Lesser men than Monet inevitably weakened the Impressionist technique. By 1907, an American art historian complained with some justice:

A vast majority of modern pictures, including many American ones, are nothing more than studies of light as it filters through muslin curtains, creeps between the slats of Venetian blinds, or in full sunshine pours over the lace caps of peasant women or the white gowns of first communicants.[51]

Even after Impressionism triumphed, many critics agreed with the conservative Frank J. Mather: 'It is become in its turn a beautiful convention . . .'.[52] Social realists, who wanted art to reflect the contemporary scene, retained a similar skepticism for different reasons. 'In the Nineties we were opposed to Impressionism, with its blue shadows and orange lights because it seemed "unreal",' John Sloan recalled. 'We chose our colors from observation of facts and qualities of *the things* we painted, with little reference to phenomena of light effects.' Distrustful of 'eyesight painting', realists 'went back to art in the direction of Manet and Goya'.[53] Impressionism's subject-matter did not seem easily adaptable to the American scene. The landscape was not cheerful; few scenes fell into a natural harmony. Foreigners often complained that 'the sky was not right in America; there was no landscape; the atmosphere was too sharp'.[54]

Impressionism inevitably provoked most hostility from conservative critics and academicians, who saw in its looseness and personal qualities more than a mere assault on discipline. The painters who prized immediacy and self-expression seemed to break radically with long-established values derived from a past that was larger than individuals or eras. The 'academic' painter's elegance and universal symbolism offered a comforting attachment to tradition amid the sudden proliferation of conflicting ideas, and the erosion of certitude in every field of endeavor.

But despite the criticism, Impression combined many appeals, and by 1900 was a reigning style in both Europe and the United States. It seemed innocent in the face of complexity, and allowed for individual expression amid increasing inter-dependence. And it permitted each viewer to create order with his own perception.

Yet Americans accepted Impression with reservations, and landscapists especially developed a muted manner. The low-keyed harmonies of autumn and winter appealed more than the cheerful, often blazing, fields and skies common in French canvases. At a show of native Impressionists in 1893, a reporter noted that the canvases were calm and self-contained, 'with none of the splendid, barbaric color that distinguishes the work of the Frenchmen. They tend to silvery greys, modified by greens and blues quite as silvery'. In 1896, another observer called J. Alden Weir's paintings 'Impressionism minus its violence. . .'.[55] Most receptive painters remained somewhat apprehensive of natural power, and emphasized man and humane values within a natural order. As a critic wrote of John H. Twachtman: 'He expressed his comprehension of the world, his ideas of man and nature, through a unified design'.[56]

Impressionism never displaced other landscape styles. His treatment of man, space, and nature made Winslow Homer more popular than formal Impressionists. Homer began as a genre painter and illustrator, but in the independent isolation of Prout's Neck, Maine, he depicted the dramatic confrontations of individuals with the elements. Homer was immensely gifted at delineating the sea's vastness, or the enveloping solitude and harmonious grandeur of snow-filled winter woods. The hunters, fisherfolk, and even the animals in his paintings were points of reference for a dominant interest in abstract natural power.

Homer's muted palette harked back to old masters, but his tone and treatment were thoroughly American. Solitary figures in the wind or on the sea symbolized individual courage against loneliness and unfathomable scope. Genre studies of fishing or the hunt were essays in space and solitude. He created a sense of both familiar reality and heroic romance in a personal style that matched the national ethos. Homer's greatest works became 'history' and allegory in symbolizing the accepted American tradition of personal freedom and courage amid natural elements.

Neither Homer nor Thomas Eakins entered the art world's debates over cosmopolitanism or 'art for art's sake', but both were aware of innovations, including the photography that was altering formal composition. Eakins painted a concert singer on stage with only the conductor's hand and baton in view. Homer often cropped objects and figures to emphasize the motion and intensity of storm in his marine paintings.

The impact of photography paralleled Japanese influence on western art. Receptive artists saw universal concepts in oriental painting's balance and detachment. The Japanese masters delineated forms with color fields rather than line, and used foreshortening and unusual juxtapositions to create perspective and motion. Calm tones and empty spaces emphasized important things left unsaid. Some Americans such as John La Farge saw innovation in Japanese painting, which still had the sanctity of a unified tradition.

All the controversial and exciting influences of Impressionism, photography, and orientalism seemed to focus on James McNeill Whistler. Born in Massachusetts into a peripatetic family, Whistler failed out of West Point, and briefly sketched maps and charts for the Coast Survey before studying in Europe. Settling in London, he became famous as a self-centered raconteur, but his dandified exoticism and sharp wit shielded a sensitive nature that was deeply committed to art.

Whistler attained fame for portraits such as those of his mother, and of Thomas Carlyle, that revealed penetrating insight. He did salon pieces, etchings, pastels and watercolors, and was an ingenious decorator. He learned a rather grave harmony from Velasquez, and an arresting tone from the Japanese. But those and other subtle influences only blended with his own major abilities.

He rejected story-telling and objective realism; the good painting was a self-contained entity. 'A picture is finished when all trace of the means used to bring about the end has disappeared', he insisted in a radical definition of the artist's mission to rise above a particular time and circumstance.[57] Whistler labelled his greatest works 'arrangements', 'nocturnes', and 'symphonies' of color to affirm their lack of realistic subject-matter. Unlike the Impressionists who thrived on sunlight, Whistler loved twilight and evening, when the world attained unity in the sumptuous mystery of shadows and blended colors:

As the light fades and the shadows deepen, all the petty and exacting details vanish, everything trivial disappears, and I see things as they are in great strong masses: the buttons are lost, but the sitter remains; the sitter is lost, but the shadow remains; the shadow is lost, but the picture remains. And that, night cannot efface from the painter's imagination.[58]

Whistler sought to evoke indistinct remembered and imagined emotions that would harmonize life's details, and his self-contained paintings had remarkable presence and dignity.

The style evoked charges of preciosity and effeteness. Critics insisted that art must instruct or 'improve' through interpreted realism and symbolism within a recognizable tradition. Whistler's waspish manner and love of controversy made it hard for many people to comprehend his general purpose, and he was ahead of the times in both taste and perception. 'There is mystery here [and] the people don't want it', he said. 'What they like is when the east wind blows, when you can look across the river and count the wires in the canary bird's cage on the other side.'[59]

A barbed but perceptive judgement, for conflicting definitions of reality lay behind the controversy around his work. Whistler found unity and interest in evocation and an enveloping imprecision; the art public found them in predictable reality. He offered a new manner of comprehending both art and the world to people who by training, taste, and custom avoided the disturbing uncertainties of abstractions. His highly individualistic work belonged to no school, but Whistler was heir to many of the world influences that undermined didacticism and academic formulas.

Like painters, sculptors enjoyed growing public support, and discussed the interactions of new ideas and lingering classical styles. Augustus St-Gaudens, J. Q. A. Ward, and other sculptors populated parks and city intersections with the statuary of heroic realism that celebrated both individual feats and national greatness. Architects, sculptors, and painters cooperated to decorate monumental buildings.

There was no lack of opportunities. Minnesota, Iowa, South Dakota, and Wisconsin commissioned new state capitols, with lavish external ornamentation and internal decoration. Expanding local government required new courthouses and office buildings. Construction of the Boston Public Library created national interest, and the federal government contributed its examples of modified European styles in the ornate Library of Congress and other buildings. Universities, private clubs, churches, and luxury hotels became monuments to a desire to modify material power with artistic decoration.

A new school of mural painters hoped to integrate buildings and their social functions with paintings that instructed the public in Justice, Liberty, and Learning. Their art did not exist 'for the benefit of any close corporation, even of artists'.[60] Recognizable allegory would improve the citizenry and advance the cause of art:

... art so directed becomes an idealized embodiment of the national life, and is brought within the reach of millions. And the benefit will react upon Art itself, since her domain is thereby widened, her opportunities increased, and an incentive supplied to higher and nobler work.[61]

Mural painting may have been 'the oldest, the most inclusive, and the most exacting of the arts', but it drew on few American examples except the derivative decorations in the national Capitol.[62] The reigning French master of the form, Puvis de Chavannes, was most successful when given a smooth, continuous surface in a self-contained area. Muralists had to understand building materials, dampness control, and lighting effects. The muralist had to 'wear wings, yet grope in subcellars'.[63] But architects usually alloted them unconnected spaces that made the finished works seem incongruous.

Subject-matter was equally baffling. Europeans accepted allegorical murals drawn from religion or a lengthy dramatic history that were both natural and instructive. But Americans had few similar unifying themes. Contemporary men and events seemed ephemeral, and the temptation was strong to employ local subjects or artificial heroics. Artists seeking respectability and unity transformed American ideals like freedom and equality into allegory, since 'few can grasp an abstract idea, but . . . a visible, tangible image is easily understood'.[64]

The confused theories, jangling array of subjects, and hasty building produced some astonishing works. The waspish Henry Blake Fuller satirized 'The Genius of the West Lighting the Way to Further Progress', and 'Science and Democracy Opening the Way for the Car of Progress' suggested as murals for a mythical Grindstone National Bank. His short story's hero outlined the ultimate combination of materialism and uplift:

'The Goddess of Finance,' in robes of saffron and purple, 'Declaring a Quarterly Dividend.' Gold background. Stockholders summoned by the Genius of Thrift blowing fit to kill on a silver trumpet. Scene takes place in an autumnal grove of oranges and pomegranates – trees loaded down with golden eagles and half-eagles. Marble pavement strewn with fallen coupons.[65]

Goddesses of Justice and Equality stared down from many courthouse walls; sugary nymphets sang Love's praises on ballroom ceilings; leather-aproned men operated the Forges of Industry in bank foyers, but muralists produced several successes. William Morris Hunt created the era's most effective murals for H. H. Richardson's new state capitol building in Albany in 1878. In two fifteen by forty-five feet panels, Hunt employed modern techniques in allegorical scenes. 'The Barque of the Discoverer' showed the feminine spirits of Faith, Hope, Fortune, and Science directing Columbus toward the New World. The brooding central figure stood against a twilight sky, an impressive evocation of enigma and hope. The opposite space contained Hunt's triumph. 'The Flight of Night', depicted Anahita, the oriental goddess of night, fleeing across the heavens before the dawn, behind a shadowy figure leading three magnificent prancing horses.

Hunt experimented for years with the theme and with new painting methods. Most murals were canvases glued to walls, but Hunt developed a temperature-resistant pigment, and outlined the figures on blank sandstone walls in paint two inches thick. This enhanced their perspective and motion against an opulent, cloud-filled background.

The murals were popular, and established a precedent for works that combined emotion and meaningful symbolism. But overwork apparently caused Hunt to commit suicide in 1879. The walls cracked, and a bracing structure covered his masterpieces. His surviving sketches revealed brilliant drawing, rich colors, and a striking sense of vastness and motion. 'The Flight of Night' was an essay in ordered majesty, and a statement of belief in the triumph of reason over error, and of grandeur over the mundane. Both works expressed great talent, and an artistic concern for unity that did not sacrifice imagination.

John La Farge created a series of impressive, if traditional, murals for several New York churches. John Singer Sargent, Edwin Austen Abbey, and Puvis de Chavannes successfully decorated the elegant new Boston Public Library in the mid 1890s. Many public buildings contained murals, but the form remained generally unimaginative. Most decorators relied on stylized allegory or shallow historical subjects which the public could easily identify. And painters were seldom able to integrate their work with a building's style or social purpose. Construction was temporary and chaotic, and murals usually seemed artificial.

The arts reflected the world's general 'state of uncertainty and experimentation',[66] and two of Thomas Eakins's paintings illustrated a generation of change. 'The Gross Clinic' of 1875 emphasized the rugged grandeur of a great individual doctor. 'The Agnew Clinic' of 1889 depicted a white-smocked surgeon directing a group enterprise, and showed how much even surgery had yielded to impersonal skilled specialists and technology.

Artistic developments involved a desire, perhaps a need, to retain an 'American' viewpoint within a larger context. They resembled other public efforts to gain the benefits of cohesion and the interchange of ideas without closing outlets for individual expression. The pull of cosmopolitanism was strong to a generation seeking the respectability to be gained from adhering to established tastes. Yet native styles remained vigorous and varied, and creative men profited from the challenges of older traditions. Cosmopolitan influences forced them to examine their own ideals, widen their scope of concern, and to use the esthetics, if not always the subject-matter, of other cultures. A deep interest in diverse artistic expressions revealed the generation's desire for fresh ways of perceiving an endlessly expanding and complex reality. A productive concern for the arts accompanied the nation's material development, and American art in turn enriched world culture.

[4]

A World Role

AFTER the Union armies disbanded in 1865, few citizens
were interested in world affairs. The growing influx of
immigrants seemed to prove that the United States was a
haven for those seeking relief from Old World rivalries.
Americans were suspicious of European power, and were
relieved not to be involved in 'imperialism'. The public and
government wanted to develop a mobile society, and to
encourage by example peoples like the Cubans who sought
self-rule.

Yet many observers understood that communications,
increased world trade, and new ideas were drawing the
nation toward involvement in world affairs. Great Britain,
France, the newly unified Germany, and a modernizing
Japan developed foreign policies through cabinet governments, relatively free from immediate popular whims and
pressures. But every American decision-maker represented
an impatient and changing constituency. Policies naturally
reflected the confusions and cross-purposes of the electorate's general attitudes. Presidents and diplomats sought to
define national interests, but a conservative Congress
thwarted any executive policy that did not coincide with
public opinion. The division between official statement and
action, and changing public moods hampered the development of any consistent diplomacy.[1]

The simple lack of accurate information and trained staff
also inhibited planners. The diplomatic corps displayed a
Jacksonian rusticity, and partisan politics figured more than
merit in making appointments. Many people considered
consular and ministerial posts 'soft berth[s] for wealthy
young men who enjoy court society'.[2] Every president im-

proved the service, but foes said it was all a waste of money. Americans who demanded expertise in economics and politics suspected a tenured diplomatic staff, the traditional preserve of artistocracies. 'What a pity it is that diplomacy is not more a career with us!' President Benjamin Harrison lamented in 1891.[3]

Congress allowed the State Department only 31 clerks in 1869. Presidential pleading increased the number to 50 in 1881, but many politicians grumbled about expanding executive power. Congress funded special bureaus only grudgingly, and experts were scarce. An elaborate new building housed the State Department across the White House lawn, but the routine inside was slow. An occasional cultural figure went to a major court, but most ministers behaved like the politicians they were. And a people always attuned to action distrusted 'channels' and the diplomat's tendency to compromise.

Europeans considered the United States a youthful giant, destined for future greatness, but awkward to live with now. Her economic might was obvious, and with coastlines facing three oceans, she could not avoid world affairs. Small signs indicated a growing tendency to take her into account. Americans attended conferences on bimetallism, postal regulations, world fairs, and copyright laws. Others explored polar wastes, South American rivers, and African jungles. The government acquired outposts that symbolized growing interests, but had no formal allies.

Secretary of State William H. Seward felt these frustrations keenly while seeking strategic and commercial expansion. He secured Alaska and Midway Island in 1867, and wanted the Danish West Indies, Santo Domingo, Cuba, Porto Rico, Greenland, Iceland, Hawaii, and an isthmian canal route. But opponents thwarted him, agreeing with an irate congressman who condemned 'one insane enough to buy the earthquakes of St Thomas and the ice fields in Greenland'.[4]

Seward's ideas were lost on a public concerned with

Reconstruction, economic development, and social problems. Despite occasional interest, the United States did not have the substance of power. A nation without a navy commanded little respect in an age of seapower, and in 1880 an officer reported acidly that the fleet resembled a paper fort painted with bellicose dragons to ward off enemies. In the mid 1880s, the Chilean fleet could ravage California. The Austrians could bombard New York. And Brazilian vessels could attack Gulf ports. Massachusetts congressman John D. Long called the navy 'an alphabet of floating washtubs'.[5] Oscar Wilde's Canterville Ghost comforted the lady who complained that her country lacked ruins and curiosities. 'No ruins! No curiosities! You have your navy and your manners!'[6]

Ships seemed to be expensive ornaments to penurious congressmen. But backward technology, an ossified officer corps more interested in social status than ideas, and lack of equipment were more to blame than politics. Only in the late 1880s did a new style of training, fresh information on naval architecture, steam power, and improved armor plate make a modern fleet possible.

Some important politicians and theorists attacked the problem during President Arthur's administration. Navies were part of diplomatic and commercial authority in a new era of competition for spheres of influence. These spokesmen were not jingoes or imperialists, but men who realized that no country would respect American interests under mere moral duress. 'What do the nations of the earth care about your moral power after you leave your own shores?' Democratic Senator Charles Jones of Florida asked in 1884. 'All that they respect when the emergency arises is a decent display of public force'.[7] National pride, new strategic needs, and a growing realization that events were changing world power arrangements concerned these men.

Many other observers disliked rising European influence, especially in Latin America. The United States was losing the ability to encourage peoples seeking independence. In 1890, New Hampshire's Republican Senator William E. Chandler protested against recalling ships from Brazil, then adopting republicanism. 'To omit to go to the River Plate is bad enough', he fumed, 'not to remain in Brazil until the new republic is organized may prove to be a crime. How many ships of European monarchies are there posted to the new republic? Shall the only republican fleet come away? What is the need of a navy?'[8]

Despite exasperation and delay, the fleet slowly improved. President Garfield's Navy Secretary, William H. Hunt, called for full reports on all aspects of operations in 1881. Secretary William E. Chandler continued this interest in administrative reform and expert skills, and in 1883, Congress authorized three steel-and-steam ships. The 'White Squadron' tested new machinery and became the pattern for a modern fleet. President Harrison's Navy Secretary, Benjamin F. Tracy, combated both spoilsmen and inertia to secure more ships, better training, and improved treatment for officers and crew. By 1896, the capital fleet ranked about sixth in world lists.

While politicians increased service appropriations, a few theorists outlined new views on national power in world affairs. After 1884, the Naval War College molded an officer corps and a new staff system. Captain A. T. Mahan's writings on the use of seapower to create diplomatic and commercial strength appealed to many important men. But jingoism did not parallel official interest in world events. No important theorist, officer, or politician favored offensive armament or an interventionist policy. Naval power seemed cheap, movable, and awesome compared to expeditionary forces. The navies that every major country developed were part of a mechanistic answer to new technology and weaponry in a shrinking world. Nations with naval bases, coaling stations, and cable landings theoretically would 'control' shipping and transit lanes. Fleets would permit imperial nations like Britain to oversee colonies cheaply. But fast, heavily armed squadrons with cable communications home could also help avoid war among major powers. The presence of rival fleets, as at Manila Bay in 1898, would signal the need for diplomatic settlement. Seapower would checkmate, not provoke.

Official concern over territorial changes seemed to accompany new interest in staff planning, education, and armaments. All parties agreed to uphold the Monroe Doctrine; the United States obviously would secure an isthmian canal route and oversee the Caribbean. Acquisition of California and Oregon in the 1840s had long since created interest in Pacific affairs. The Hawaiian Islands' strategic and commercial importance in mid Pacific were obvious, and foreign observers assumed the United States would annex them if the weak native monarchy fell or if foreign influence increased. And sporadic efforts to secure Caribbean bases were a sidelight to the persistent Cuban problem. But no presidential candidate discussed foreign affairs to an electorate concerned chiefly with currency reform, tariff protection, and national development.

The interest in territory was more apparent than real. Secretary of State Bayard promoted a multi-power settlement in Samoa, but he and successors served notice of a developing American *presence*. Except for obvious concern about the Caribbean and Hawaii, they did not seek colonies. The United States hoped to function among European powers with consent rather than force, but policy-planners watched developments closely. A dynamic and rapidly industrializing Japan seemed the chief future Pacific rival. An often ill-mannered Germany was eager for world power. Count Bismarck was a hero to many Americans who approved blood and iron in the service of national unity and economic stability, but German expansion was another matter. 'That Germany has of late years given evidence of a disposition to cherish schemes of distant annexation and civilization in many quarters of the globe seems unquestionable . . .' Bayard wrote confidentially in 1885.[9] Sober men like Connecticut's Republican Senator Orville H. Platt knew the United States could not escape some new demands, however distasteful:

... we ought not to adopt any land-getting policy, but the greed of acquiring territory has so fastened on all European states. It is a fever, a disease, a craze. How long will it be before the European powers will turn covetous eyes westward, and how soon we shall be compelled either to abandon the Monroe Doctrine or fight in its defense no one knows. England has about every strategic point in the world of consequence but the Sandwich Islands [Hawaii]. I don't relish the idea of her getting that one.[10]

Few people wanted territory, but new thinking about ocean strategy, growing national pride, and a fresh expansionist rationale helped shape an attitude toward the world.

Inexperience made minor crises like the Samoa incident seem important to a few American diplomats and naval officers, but they did not create popular interest in foreign affairs in the 1880s. At most, articulate men warned of emerging challenges. But the new outlook was not accidental; no one forced it on the United States. Concern about world politics rose naturally from the pattern of national development. A long history of continental expansion would make acquiring overseas territory seem logical. Men who went to California naturally became concerned about what lay beyond the water's edge, especially when new navies closed the distance between land masses.

James G. Blaine's 'Pan-Americanism' encompassed most of his countrymen's assumptions about the world. The brilliant but controversial 'Man From Maine' became secretary of state in 1881 both to formulate foreign policy and to help President Garfield liberalize the GOP. Blaine guarded America's prerogatives, but was aware of her limitations. He wanted to expand overseas markets, and realized that voters would credit his party with new prestige, but he was not an annexationist. It was a frustrating job for the nervous and imaginative Blaine. Only a politician with his popular following could dramatize a new departure or long-term planning, but political enemies attacked anything he suggested. At best, he could outline new procedures for dull successors, and create some public support.

Blaine was anti-British, and suspected that nation's ambitions south of the border. He wished to renegotiate the Clayton-Bulwer Treaty to permit United States control of an isthmian canal. But delay in London and squabbling in Central America stalled negotiations, while foes laid down a barrage of newspaper criticism against his 'jingoism'. President Garfield's assassination in July 1881 threw the Secretary's future into doubt, and the new president, Chester A. Arthur, was a political antagonist.

The canal was only a step in Blaine's grand design to develop a stable Latin America oriented toward the United States. But he became embroiled in a rancorous Chilean quarrel that illustrated the disruptive role of partisan politics in diplomacy. Chile was of special interest to Washington. Her nitrate and guano resources were promises of future power, but invited both quarrels with neighbors and foreign intervention. British and French technicians supervised mineral extraction, and foreign officers trained the armed forces. Her small modern fleet theoretically could devastate San Francisco and put Chile's flag in the Pacific.

Misinformation and weak subordinates drew Blaine into the 'War of the Pacific', a running fight between Chile and Peru. Critics quickly attacked his larger plan for hemispheric cooperation. He wanted to convene the American states and at least outline an arbitration system to prevent economic disruption and political instability. If the United States evaded this duty, Europeans would enter by default. 'The United States cannot play between nations the part of the dog in the manger'.[11]

This 'Pan-American' system blended the self-interest, moralism, and faith in progress that animated most American policies. Established rules of conduct and emotional ties would steadily enlarge the area's wealth, and provide a market for United States goods while Latins developed their own economies. More subtle, long-lasting forces would accompany the panoply of treaties and conferences. A common system of coinage, weights, and measures; free travel and trade; and educational exchange would keep the New World 'liberal'. The proposal reflected Blaine's concept of American self-interest, and the era's hopes and values. It bespoke a profound belief in the social benefits of material well-being, and assumed that a rational system would divert national passions to a larger good.

But President Arthur shortly withdrew the invitations to a conference in Washington. He hesitated to inaugurate bold ventures without a political mandate. The plan also would require congressional cooperation on dangerous subjects like tariff reciprocity, the diplomatic service, executive authority, and armaments. Blaine left the cabinet in December 1881. The President proceeded undramatically and piecemeal, but was no isolationist. He was suspicious of the proposed international organization, whose weak members could collectively outvote the United States. He supported naval modernization, and sought commercial expansion through individual treaties. But neither style of Pan-Americanism won the day. The Senate ignored a group of commercial agreements as Arthur left office in March 1885.

Observers expected Blaine to resume these labors as secretary of state for President Harrison in 1889. Debate and events seemed to produce a better atmosphere, and the departing Cleveland administration arranged for a congress of American states. Delegates gathered in the fall of 1889, and toured the country. Prominent educators, editors, and publicists praised their earnest discussions of patent regulations and arbitration. President Harrison emphasized trade by appointing four manufacturers and two merchants to a ten-man United States delegation. He and Blaine also helped secure a reciprocity section in the McKinley Tariff of 1890. A protectionist Congress only grudgingly allowed the president to penalize the goods of Latin American nations that did not accord equal treatment to United States imports. But even this negative reciprocity was an expandable beginning. Republicans like Blaine and McKinley hoped to use reciprocity for commercial advantage, and to develop economic stability in the hemisphere.

But events once more defeated Blaine's policy. The misconduct of American sailors in Valparaiso created an outburst of Chilean resentment that almost provoked war. Though Blaine actually restrained Harrison, foes raised the old 'jingo!' cry. The world press criticized American overreaction, and seconded Chilean resentment of 'yankee imperialism'. Arbitration settled the issue, but American influence waned. An ailing Blaine left office in June 1892, and Harrison's defeat that November ended official interest in Pan-Americanism. The long effort to develop hemispheric cooperation revealed the difficulty of dealing with neighbors. Societies perpetually in transition or threatened with disorder created endless political factions that could not be appeased. Whatever the United States did, including inaction, was wrong. And sensitive Latins inevitably saw her as a threat, not an example, whom they opposed in order to define their own nationalistic purposes.

The failure to attain Pan-Americanism illustrated the difficulties of formulating coherent policy in a representative political system. Congress opposed any diplomacy involving economic risks. Legislators slowly funded a new Navy that appealed to national pride, and seemed purely defensive, but they would not subsidize a new merchant marine, which was necessary to let businessmen compete in foreign markets. A few Republicans like Blaine and McKinley promoted tariff reciprocity as a way of extending influence without diplomatic confrontations. They were interested in commercial expansion, but sought beneficial long-term world stability more than immediate profits. But congressmen protected the home market, and regularly defeated the men interested in overseas trade. The desire for commercial expansion motivated a few politicians and businessmen, but it was not the driving force of American foreign policy.

Some statesmen and thinkers were ahead of popular opinion as the 1880s closed, but they could only watch events and propagandize. The public usually practiced an automatic patriotism. The British minister's inept comments on the presidential canvass of 1888 provoked an insular anti-British indignation. Politicians aroused voters over Canadian violations of territorial waters, occasional Mexican bandit raids, and imported Chinese laborers. But specific reactions did not constitute a well developed foreign policy.

Yet the American people automatically accepted several beliefs about the nation's historical role, to which any president had to fit a rational policy. They considered the United States a force for both liberalism and stability. Her mere concern about overseas events would somehow temper conservative European influence. Her opinion, if not her might, would promote local self-rule patterned after American examples. A rising standard of living under western tutelage would develop both individual freedom and collective responsibility. Enlightened laws that recognized the freedom to compete would prevent revolutions, and give all nations in an area material interests to protect, thus enhancing their desire to compromise volatile national issues.

This ill-defined and subtly contradictory rhetoric seemed radical, but the United States was committed to the essentially conservative goal of a stable world order. Even in the 1890s, her interests resembled those of the 'great powers' more than the emerging peoples she sought to encourage. Historic American rhetoric sounded revolutionary, but merely espoused representative self-government and individualism, which were often ill-suited to other peoples. The public never perceived ironies in this body of attitudes. Politicians automatically unified opinion by combining 'duty' and American power. Cynical foreign diplomats and 'native' peoples saw a gap between words and deeds that escaped Americans. Few Americans doubted that others would follow their example; fewer still anticipated disruptive nationalism that failed to distinguish between 'conservative' Europeans and 'liberal' Americans. In time, all foreigners became 'imperialists' to emerging peoples, and the American public then talked of ingratitude and 'backwardness'.

The desire to alleviate suffering, destroy autocracy, and promote an undefined but moving 'liberalism' reflected inexperience in power relations and the optimism of a pluralistic society that built a new industrial economy in one generation. But the hope of finding a middle path between emerging peoples and 'imperialists' also illustrated the era's lack of alternatives to national power. No agency or method existed to assist 'native' people except through investment, and technology drawn from foreigners, who inevitably overestimated the viability of an imperial system.

The 1890s brought a subtle sense of change, a feeling that national unity was at last a reality. Industrialism would obviously triumph, as part of an integrated world economy that required stability for prosperity. Many Americans sought a larger 'civilizing' mission beyond material success to sustain national vitality. The historian Frederick Jackson Turner noted the human psyche's apparent need for expansive goals. The frontier's disappearance might create public concern about the Pacific Basin, which was only 'the logical outcome of the nation's march to the Pacific'.[12]

Similar concern about national purpose flavored the writings of clergymen and educators, who reached an increasingly literate public through magazines, newspapers, and subscription book lists. They discussed a sharpened sense of the duty to extend humanitarian Christianity throughout the world. Despite its condescension, 'uplift' would prepare 'native' peoples for future responsibility. It sought to 'civilize' indirectly through missionaries and traders who brought both goods and news of an outside world that was increasingly concerned about events in 'dark' Africa and 'enigmatic' Asia. The doctrine was generally more cultural than racist, assuming that technology and a rising living standard made western culture superior to that of tropical peoples. Tutelage would ease under-developed nations into the world order.

The anti-expansionists who feared contamination from tropical peoples were the era's most prominent racists. Industrialism and science proved with a vengeance that change was the fundamental law of life. The very peoples whom westerners confronted in Africa and Asia slumbered in the false belief that isolation from the outside world was permanent. There was no way to embargo ideas, the spirit of adventure, the search for profit, or the compulsion to convert. No government could forbid the export of ideas, or stifle new systems of communication that circled the globe. Expansionists wished to avoid stagnation, and temper the process of modernization for the security and long-term stability of everyone involved. Some vital dynamic in human life made great powers seek influence and authority everywhere. Expansionism thus combined western man's apprehensions about a coming rearrangement of power and his faith in human ability to blend cultures without threatening freedom.

A generation of optimists unified the argument with a genuine sense of responsibility, so easily labelled 'duty'. Many Americans agreed with Goldwin Smith that 'the youth of the American Republic is over; maturity, with its burdens, its difficulties, and its anxieties has come'.[13] The sobering biological simile of youth exchanging freedom for adult responsibilities occurred often in expansionist writings. These doctrines and attitudes reached the masses in diluted form, and people often used them after the event to rationalize a reaction, but they added a sense of grandeur to personal beliefs. Intangible feelings about destiny, duty, and national purpose sometimes actually undermined material self-interest, but were inevitably important to a generation seeking unity and stability amid unprecedented change.

As the century neared its end, the public discussed domestic policies. Tariff reform gave the conservative

Grover Cleveland a second term in 1892. Politicians worried
about a 'Populist Revolt' among agrarians dissatisfied with
industrialism. Depression, the violent Pullman Strike, and
the organized protest of 'Coxey's Army' in 1894 provoked
momentary fears of social disorder. The nation's ideals
promoted unity, but these strains and stresses also sharpened
feelings that the United States must encourage freedom
while pursuing material well-being.

A few crises illustrated the new proximity of foreign
events. In 1893, the departing Harrison administration
submitted a treaty annexing the new Republic of Hawaii.
But Cleveland opposed territorial acquisitions, criticized
unofficial American support for the men who overthrew the
monarchy, and repudiated the agreement in order to
embarrass the Republican party. Yet he wished to maintain
informal dominion in both Hawaii and Latin America
through trade and diplomacy. In 1895, he forced Great
Britain to arbitrate a dispute with Venezuela, and firmly
asserted the United States' dominant role in the hemisphere.
He also faced a Cuban war that inflamed public feeling and
involved national self-interests. And while he was not pro-
Cuban, Cleveland warned Spain to end the conflict quickly
or face American intervention.

Conditions in the 'Ever-Faithful Isle' had long typified
everything the Monroe Doctrine allegedly sought to prevent, and Americans took pleasure in periodic Cuban revolts
against Spanish misrule. The 'Ten Years' War' of 1868–78
set a pattern of American reaction against Spanish in-
transigence, and against guerilla warfare that did not
differentiate between soldiers and 'innocent' civilians. Despite several tense crises over Spanish violations of American
citizenship, the Grant administration avoided war. Spain
secured a paper peace with the rebels in 1878 that only
damped the fires of war. Suffering Cuba was part of the
American consciousness long before 1898. No sudden or
accidental 'yellow press' campaign created public demands
to free the island.

Lavish expenditures of men and money revealed Spain's pride in her last major possession. By 1896, some 150,000 soldiers had served in Cuba; by 1898, disease and warfare had killed or disabled about 100,000. Casualties among the ill-armed *insurrectos* were proportionately higher, and Americans cheered the under-dog. In New York and Miami, *juntas* of exiled Cubans fed information and propaganda to influential politicians and newsmen. But the policy of 'reconcentrating' non-combatants in towns while Spanish soldiers devastated the rebellious countryside shocked the public, and disgust with guerilla warfare ran through all levels of society. 'I do not want war', the normally detached Senator Henry Cabot Lodge wrote a friend in 1896. 'I do not want to annex the island, but I do want to see the conditions now existing in Cuba, which are a disgrace to civilization, to be brought to an end'.[14] This disregard for human life rapidly personified the abstraction of Spanish colonialism.

Those with material interests joined the chorus against 'barbarism'. Cuba's trade declined by two thirds in five years. Spanish officials mistreated Cubans with United States citizenship, stopped vessels on the high seas, and destroyed foreign property. Investors found the rebellion disastrous as both rebels and Spaniards fired cane fields, dismantled rolling mills, killed livestock, and destroyed public works. Disease and malnutrition increased the human toll. Many spokesmen thought the United States had the right and duty to expel Spain, and to dominate the approaches to an isthmian canal. Others hoped to establish a model Cuban republic that would inspire other Latins restless under autocratic traditions. Senator Lodge summed up a growing fear among cautious but realistic men that inaction would increase European power in the hemisphere. 'One reason for which we fought our war [in 1776] was that we might not have the countries side by side on this continent armed to the teeth with great armies and navies', he wrote in 1895. 'If we permit Europe to enter and parcel out

South America, if we allow England to take Cuba, we must become a great military nation. Do you think that desirable? I do not'.[15]

Congress always sounded more extreme than the Executive branch, which formulated policy. Politicians advertised Cuba's cause and threatened party disorder, but President Cleveland adopted strict neutrality as the insurrection dragged on. The navy hunted filibusters taking arms and supplies from Florida, and administration spokesmen discouraged new investments in Cuba. The President refused to accord the rebels belligerent status, lest this raise their hopes of material aid.

Cleveland coldly ignored congressional opinion, but understood the importance of trade, strategy, and political stability. 'That the United States cannot contemplate with complacency another ten years of Cuban insurrection, with all its injurious and distressing incidents, may certainly be taken for granted', Secretary of State Richard Olney formally warned Madrid on 4 April 1896.[16] Though burdened with domestic troubles, Cleveland steadily pressed Spain to speed up pacification, even in his last annual message of 1896: 'The spectacle of the utter ruin of an adjoining country, by nature one of the most fertile and charming on the globe, would engage the serious attention of the government and people of the United States in any circumstance.' Though not wishing to commit the new McKinley administration, he noted coolly '. . . The United States is not a nation to which peace is a necessity . . .' Cleveland thus established attitudes which no successor could ignore. The election of 1896 settled the nation's chief domestic issues; Cuba could now dominate public discussion.

On 4 March 1897, William McKinley inherited a Cuban problem with special scope and dynamism in American life. Accumulated tensions, policies, and attitudes limited his options and control of events. He knew the depths of popular feeling against Spain, and understood that newspaper stories only reinforced existing attitudes. As an experienced politician, he followed the press coverage, but would not bow to manufactured hysteria. But reportage intensified constituent pressure on congressmen, and weakened public perspective. No part of his constituency was firmly Republican, and political disaster would follow the failure to solve the problem. Important special interest groups were divided, but would unite if events undermined the search for a peaceful settlement. Except for Cuban investors and a few men concerned about overseas markets, the business community feared that war would interrupt returning prosperity.[17] But influential 'expansionists', such as the publisher Whitelaw Reid, seacoast congressmen and senators, and publicists like Theodore Roosevelt and Captain Mahan were prominent in Republican circles. Much of the religious community put new emphasis on missions, and educators discussed America's role in a steadily shrinking world community. The President did not read abstruse articles or thick books, but knew he confronted a changed world-view that combined emotional attitudes and newly defined self-interest.

A legendary charm made McKinley popular and politically effective. His undramatic style of leadership rested on tireless appeals for unity, skill at compromise, and the patience to hear out critics. Dislike of the limelight and love of dissimulation screened a stubborn personality that seldom yielded to pressure. Despite his apparent regard for every visitor's advice, McKinley was remarkably self-contained. Theodore Roosevelt was a trifle harsh, but basically correct in telling a friend: 'The President only loves one thing in the whole world, and that is his wife. . . . He treats everyone with equal favor; their worth to him is solely dependent on the advantages he could derive from them. . . . .'.[18]

McKinley won the presidency on domestic issues, but had worked with Blaine and Harrison for Pan-Americanism, accepted the need for naval power, and wanted tariff reciprocity. He was interested in expanding overseas

markets, but was a typical American in reacting against mis-
government, cruelty, and instability. Though not identified
with territorial expansion, he understood the strategic
thinking behind the movement to annex Hawaii and dominate the Caribbean. He was as knowledgeable about foreign
affairs as any new president. While he naturally accepted
prevailing values, he was flexible, open to compromise, and
on speaking terms with nearly every important public man.
His talent for compromise reflected a personal aversion to
strife, and a commitment to Christian ideals. But McKinley
was pre-eminently a political realist, desiring order and
organized development, and he was determined to end the
Cuban problem. He would be patient, ready to compromise,
and would exhaust every diplomatic possibility. If that
failed, he would intervene.

McKinley's love of indirection and refusal to discuss
diplomacy publicly blurred both his policy and personal
role. He accepted the unwritten limitations on presidential
leadership, and would not risk creating tensions in the
complicated political structure by seeking popularity. Like
any policy maker, he realized that unpredictable events
could swiftly undermine the loftiest or most cautious pro-
nouncements. Anything he might say would increase
divisive speculation, promote rancorous debate, and weaken
his influence. He attended closely to details, and quickly
mastered the available information, but a willingness to
credit others often made him seem to lack force. Elihu Root,
later his secretary of war, understood this method of controlling men with ceremonial rewards. 'He was a man of
great power because he was absolutely indifferent to credit',
Root said. 'His desire was "to get it done". He cared nothing
about credit, but McKinley always had his way.'[19]

The President could only indirectly control an impatient
and jealous Congress, which was a clearing-house for
rhetoric and plans concerning Cuba. 'Czar' Reed dominated the Republican House, but the Senate was still badly
divided over free silver and Populism. Fourteen years in the

House had taught McKinley the byways of congressional influence. Senators would rebel at either overt executive pressure or inattention, as they had just done with Cleveland. This was especially true in making foreign policy, a constitutional preserve they jealously shared with the strongest president. As Senator George F. Hoar succinctly noted: 'The most eminent senators would have received as a personal affront a private message from the White House expressing a desire that they should adopt any course in the discharge of their legislative duties that they did not approve. If they visited the White House, it was to give, not to receive advice'.[20] So the President had to risk the delays, gossip, and personal misunderstandings inherent in any indirect approach, and worked through agents like Hanna, Aldrich, and Lodge. All were moderates on intervention; but each knew exactly the support he could command for any act. McKinley added a personal touch by keeping open house, treating all visitors to confidence and respect, and mixing with critics at social functions.

McKinley had difficulty in finding experienced diplomatic agents. He retained Fitzhugh Lee in the crucial Havana consulate, who despite well known pro-Cuban sympathies, was experienced and responsible. The President wanted a moderate for the ministry in Madrid, but remarked significantly that 'if nothing could be done with Spain, he desired to show that he had spared no effort to avert trouble'.[21] Stewart Woodford, prominent New York lawyer and Republican, took the thankless task in September 1897. Within the administration, McKinley relied on an old Ohio friend, William R. Day, assistant secretary of state, and the real power behind the figurehead Secretary, John Sherman.

The President also wanted information about conditions in Cuba, which fully accredited officials could not likely obtain. In June 1897, he dispatched a political confidant, William J. Calhoun of Illinois, to survey the scene. Calhoun talked to Spaniards and Cubans, visited reconcentration

sites, and toured the countryside. His private report to
McKinley emphasized Lee's long-held conclusions: Spain
could neither pacify the island nor grant genuine self-rule.
Powerful home interests feared the political effects of a
settlement that acceded to American demands. Influential
men of Spanish descent who dominated Cuba were equally
intractable. And the rebels believed the United States would
ultimately intervene if warfare continued. So Cuba slipped
steadily into chaos:

> I travelled by rail from Havana to Matanzas. The country out-
> side of the military posts was practically depopulated. Every
> house had been burned, banana trees cut down, cane fields swept
> with fire, and everything in the shape of food destroyed. It was as
> fair a landscape as mortal eye ever looked upon; but I did not see
> a house, man, woman, or child, a horse, mule, or cow, nor even a
> dog. I did not see a sign of life, except an occasional vulture or
> buzzard sailing through the air. The country was wrapped in the
> stillness of death and the silence of desolation.

The war would continue until Spain was bankrupt or an
outside power intervened. Whatever happened, peace
would find Cuba devastated.[22]

The President saw little room for fresh approaches. He
understood Spain's pride and self-interest, but briefly
thought of buying the island. 'If we must lose the island of
Cuba, we would rather, believe me, lose it with honor after
a disastrous war, than through a cowardly abdication', was
a typical response which came to McKinley's desk from *Le
Temps* in Paris.[23] The administration sought a compromise
solution; Cuba must become autonomous within the
Spanish empire. Woodford thought this naturally appealed
more to Americans than to Spaniards. 'I doubt whether the
Spanish official mind comprehends real autonomy as
Englishmen and Americans would understand [it]. I doubt
whether Spain could give in theory or enforce in fact such
autonomy as Canada has.'[24]

Recognizing its dangers, McKinley adopted a tactic of
pushing Spain toward piecemeal reform. A formal note of

26 June 1897 outlined his basic demands: an end to reconcentration, aid to refugees, law and order, and autonomy.
While conceding Spain's right to pacify Cuba, McKinley
strongly reaffirmed its special relation to the United States
and deplored 'uncivilized' warfare. Only steady progress
toward autonomy would prevent intervention. The dangers
were clear: Spain might fight to avoid humiliation, and the
rebels might prolong the warfare to insure intervention.

Madrid's reply in August was not reassuring. Spain
denied any special relationship between the United States
and Cuba, reserved the right to prosecute the war with any
means, and insisted that the rebels must seek an armistice.
Spain would not modify her aims or methods; she was even
less likely to attain her goals. In September, Woodford reported gloomily that he saw no Spanish policy. Spain was
poor, divided and sullen, but clung to imperial prestige.
Specific financial and military interests adamantly opposed
concessions. Politicians feared that loss of Cuba would
provoke civil war, or topple the monarchy. The President's
desire to mediate the conflict was hopeless. Spain would
play the cards of delay, with 'a hand to mouth policy'.[25]

But the assassination that fall of the Conservative
premier, Antonio Cánovas del Castillo, brought a Liberal
ministry to power which seemed open to some American
demands. The new government quickly agreed to recall
General Valeriano Weyler, assist refugees, and develop an
autonomy plan. But it rejected American participation
except through relief agencies. Woodford was briefly optimistic, realizing prophetically that any backward step
would destroy faith in Spain's promises. In late November
1897, the Queen Regent promulgated the autonomy
decrees, but American analysts were disappointed. Spain
would retain ultimate authority in a reorganized government; the army would remain a force in Cuba. Rebels
rejected the program, and McKinley later admitted his
own disappointment. Still, any concessions were a step
forward.

A restless Congress heard clerks read McKinley's annual
message on 6 December 1897. Radical members resented his
modest success; no middle course would actually free Cuba
and oust Spain from the Caribbean. The message listed
diplomatic accomplishments, but the President remained
both firm and skeptical. If 'a righteous' peace did not come
quickly, 'the exigency of further and other action by the
United States will remain to be taken'. Jingoes naturally
thought the policy was 'cowardly, heartless and idiotic', but
the public and moderate leaders would follow the President's
lead while hope of a peaceful settlement remained.[26]
McKinley did not answer critics, but knew that every
success created fresh demands for speed in order to keep
moderate opinion from swinging to interventionism. He
would have appreciated the appeal for patience which
Senator Lodge wrote a friend:

> I do not feel that you are just to the President in regard to Cuba.
> By the firm attitude which he has assumed he forced the with-
> drawal of Weyler, the release of all the American prisoners, the
> revocation of the concentration edict. . . . Spain having made all
> these concessions, he would hardly say that they should not have
> the opportunity to try to pacify the island by autonomy, and I
> think he has acted wisely in so doing.[27]

Yet realists knew that Spain had merely promised to do
certain things. The force of royal decrees against reconcentration weakened in the hands of army officers. Spaniards
obviously clung to the delusion that one more full campaign
season would exhaust the rebels. Delay would yet produce
victory. The new year's events quickly hardened American
public opinion and official attitudes toward Spanish
promises. Madrid's rhetorical acceptance of autonomy
angered the *peninsulares* who controlled Cuba's economy and
society. 'Yankee' pressure only fortified their stubborn
opposition to any compromise. On 12 January, ex-soldiers,
hoodlums, and radicals attacked Havana newspapers and
businesses whose owners favored autonomy. Early reports
of widespread destruction and loss of life were exaggerated,

but Minister de Lôme encountered coolness at the State
Department and White House. The disorders significantly
undermined official belief in both Spain's promises and her
ability to invoke change. De Lôme noted a 'deep disgust
among the moderates and those disposed to accommodate
differences'.[28] In Madrid, Woodford bluntly warned
against a reversion to Weyler's methods. But whatever the
press and politicians said or thought, the riots ended hope
for autonomy. Too many entrenched interests in Cuba and
Spain preferred ceremonial war to change. And the Cuban
rebels now wanted full independence.

Late in January, the President reassured Minister de
Lôme of his determination to continue the search for peace.
A sensational incident shortly revealed the Minister's true
feelings, and marked another step toward war. In December
1897, de Lôme wrote a friend touring Cuba the details of
McKinley's pacific annual message, and analyzed the prospects for settlement. Cuban spies noted the return address,
and forwarded the indiscreet letter to the New York *junta*,
which let the New York *Journal* print a front-page facsimile
on 9 February 1898.

To outraged readers, the document's importance lay in
de Lôme's insulting characterization of McKinley as 'weak
and a bidder for the admiration of the crowd, besides being
a would-be politician who tries to leave a door open behind
himself while keeping on good terms with the jingoes of his
party'. But these insults interested McKinley's advisers less
than de Lôme's other observations. He suggested that
Madrid seek a reciprocity treaty to ease tension, and dis-
patch an experienced lobbyist 'to carry on propaganda
among the Senators and others in opposition to the junta
and to try to win over the refugees'. He was contemptuous
of the rebels, thought negotiation was pointless, and hoped
interest in autonomy would give the army another full
season to end the insurrection. The letter's meaning was
clear: Whether through political divisions or false intent,
Spanish promises were worthless.[29]

Secretly informed of the pending disaster, de Lôme picked up his passport before the story broke. The President naturally did not comment, but Madrid angered many people by only grudgingly disavowing the Minister's words, noting coolly that they were in a private letter stolen from the mails. Niceties of protocol really did not matter. Moderates had praised McKinley's patience and tact, but now thought war inevitable. A year of diplomacy had produced nothing but promises, while the destruction of Cuba proceeded apace. And Madrid was truculent, and disinclined to further paper concessions; Spanish officials loftily suggested that McKinley silence the New York *junta* as a sign of reciprocal amenity.

Then on the evening of 15 February, cables brought the news that the battleship *Maine* had blown up in Havana, killing 260 sailors. The *Maine* was on a courtesy visit; Spanish vessels were to call at American ports, which would hopefully ease tensions. Angry politicians, editors, and common folk now assumed that Spanish saboteurs had mined the ship, and demanded intervention to end the situation that required the vessel's presence.

McKinley still refused to quell public outrage, and hoped to remain above factions when war came. But he secured a $50,000,000 defense appropriation, most of which went to the navy. This sign of determination and wealth might shock Spain into arbitration. A commission of experts hurried to Havana to examine the wreck, and the State Department outlined its last compromise formula. Spain must grant an armistice, end reconcentration, undertake massive relief, and permit McKinley to arbitrate if no solution emerged by 1 October 1898.

Madrid now understood that only Cuban independence would satisfy the United States. On 31 March, she agreed to adopt relief measures, implement autonomy, and discuss the *Maine*'s destruction, which American experts assigned to an undefined 'external cause'. But she would not accept arbitration or recognize the rebels. McKinley turned to writing a war message. On 9 April, allegedly in response to papal pressure, Madrid granted an armistice. But McKinley correctly saw this as another delaying tactic, and merely appended it to his request for a war declaration on 11 April.

This final cease-fire offer marked no change of policy. Spain still spurned American mediation, and obviously lacked the means and desire either to end the war or grant workable autonomy. She rejected Cuban independence outright. Nothing in Spain's past performance or present capabilities warranted further trust in either her intentions or capacities. Not even his critics took this last gesture seriously, and McKinley no longer believed Spanish promises. No historical evidence showed that he was wrong. Only two solutions were open: the war could continue indefinitely and utterly destroy Cuba, or the United States could intervene. Even if Spain suppressed the insurrection after more years of conflict, the devastated island and suffering populace would concern any future administration in Washington. Patience and diplomacy had only justified evicting Spain from the hemisphere.[30]

McKinley's silence made him seem to 'capitulate' to public demands for war, but he merely accepted the final truth of what he always feared: compromise was hopeless, and only war would both save Cuba and fulfill the United States' Caribbean policy. Had he defined this position publicly in 1897, and certainly in the emotional crises of 1898, he might have improved his historical reputation, but would not have prevented war.

The American people fought primarily for humanitarian reasons, to end suffering and to secure representative self-government for Cuba. Monarchist, authoritarian Spain was the ideal foe of 'liberal' idealists. But the administration also wanted to drive Spain from the hemisphere. A free Cuba might become the model for all Latin Americans seeking freedom.

The three-month war which followed did nothing to weaken the country's confidence in its power or purpose.

But while an impatient public watched Cuba, events in Asia took the United States into world politics. In the fall of 1897, McKinley routinely approved an order sending Commodore George Dewey's fleet to Hong Kong, to strike at the Philippines if war came. On 1 May Dewey sank the Spanish fleet in Manila Bay, and became the war's first hero.

The public cheered, but politicians faced the question of what to do with the archipelago. Newspaper editors began combining 'duty' and 'opportunity'. A sharp sense of national pride, and suspicion of British, German, Japanese, and Russian designs helped create expansionist sentiment. Few people had favored war for territory, but now they expected pragmatic statesmen to seize opportunities.

McKinley said little about the Philippines, but dispatched a land force to occupy the city of Manila before Dewey's victory was confirmed. By June, he allowed visitors to persuade him of expansion's virtues and the necessities of the hour. But he was already committed to retaining the islands, and merely spent the summer developing support. He quickly diverted the cabinet from seeking only Luzon or Manila, and secured a congressional resolution annexing Hawaii. Officials talked about consummating Blaine's policies, and of developing a new Asia. The State Department hastily forbade any discussion with Filipino insurgents about future relations with the United States. The army occupied Cuba, and the navy sank Spain's Atlantic squadron. An armistice agreement on 12 August left disposition of the Philippines to peace conferees, which subtly illustrated the administration's commitment to expansion. Postponement would inevitably develop public demands to retain the islands.

McKinley did not consider attending the peace conference in Paris, but the commission he sent revealed his political skill. The moderate ex-Secretary Day as chairman would implement the President's wishes. Whitelaw Reid, publisher of the New York *Tribune*, represented expansionists in general. Ignoring some protests that senators could not approve their own handiwork, McKinley named Maine's William P. Frye, and Minnesota's Cushman K. Davis, chairman of the Foreign Relations Committee. The presence of George Gray, anti-expansionist Democrat from Delaware, would mute charges of a packed body.

While these carefully selected negotiators awaited instructions in Paris, politicians talked to McKinley about pride and power. Religious leaders discussed the opportunity to spread the gospel. Diplomats worried about the effect on world peace of abandoning the islands. Some commentators saw in Manila another Hong Kong, a trading base away from the dangerous mainland. Available information indicated that Emilio Aguinaldo's insurgents could not control or govern the islands; civil war would provoke foreign intervention if the United States departed.

In October, McKinley toured the Midwest, ostensibly to speak at the Trans-Mississippi Exposition in Omaha, but chiefly to develop opinion and help Republican congressional candidates. He talked of markets, duty, pride, and received a tumultuous reception. Back in Washington, he closed the options, and instructed the commissioners to demand the entire archipelago. An honest sense of obligation to the Filipinos, fear of foreign conflict over the islands, the prospect of new trade, and a strong feeling of destiny shaped the decision. And while he anticipated a sharp contest for Senate approval of the treaty, McKinley did not expect to fight the insurgent Filipinos.

The peace commissioners returned in mid December, and the President marshalled his forces. Most Republican senators would follow him, though a few like George F. Hoar and Eugene Hale opposed territorial expansion. Some Democrats would support the treaty to end the war; others attacked 'McKinley imperialism'. Only the most careful executive leadership could produce the necessary two-thirds vote in such a divided body.

A varied collection of people fought the treaty. Andrew Carnegie feared that empire would make the United States

aristocratic, and erode individualism. He spoke harsh words
to McKinley's face. 'He threatens the President, not only
with the vengeance of the voters, but with practical
punishment at the hands of the mob', Secretary of State
John Hay wrote after a stormy interview with the steel
magnate.[31] Speaker Reed opposed expansion, largely on
racist grounds. So did ex-President Cleveland, partly because it reversed his own earlier policies. Intellectuals and
mugwumps like Mark Twain, E. L. Godkin, Carl Schurz,
and other 'little Americans' feared that empire would produce armaments and diplomatic confrontations. Hoar
argued that it was unconstitutional to acquire territory not
intended for statehood, or to rule dependent peoples without
their consent.

But the anti-expansionists' motives were not altogether
logical or lofty. Hoar wanted to annex Hawaii because he
thought its people welcomed the step, but opposed taking
the Philippines because its people allegedly did not approve.
The constitutional argument lapsed in the case of Puerto
Rico, now a war indemnity. The principle of annexation
was not so doubtful as the territory acquired. Increased
authority in Latin America seemed natural, but dangerous
in an unfamiliar Asia. Other critics thought the United
States should become 'the great neutral power of the world',
influential through commercial supremacy, technology, and
liberal example.[32] Public fervor also reinforced mugwump
suspicions of democracy. Would not glamorous pro-consuls,
garlanded with honors and exotic associations gained from
colonial rule, captivate a credulous electorate?

Most anti-expansionists were candid racists, who dreaded
the prospect of bringing tropical peoples into the American
system. 'No matter whether they are fit to govern themselves or not', Missouri's Democratic Representative Champ
Clark said of the Filipinos, 'they are not fit to govern us'.[33]
He also depicted future humiliations of the Congress:

How can we endure our shame when a Chinese senator from
Hawaii, with his pigtail hanging down his back, with his pagan

joss in his hand, shall rise from his curule chair and in pidgeon English proceed to chop logic with GEORGE FRISBIE HOAR or HENRY CABOT LODGE? O tempora, O mores![34]

The expansionists' motives were clearer and more appealing to the public. The United States should behave like a great power, though this did not mean imperial competition. Proponents of the 'large policy' agreed that coaling stations, naval bases, and a fleet would suffice to exercise diplomatic influence. Island outposts seemed only a logical extension of the nation's historic continentalism. The British example of apparent control through a Gibraltar-Malta-Suez-Aden-India-Singapore-Hong Kong chain appealed to American planners. They envisaged a similar line running from the east coast to a Cuban naval base, then to an isthmian canal, across to Hawaii-Guam-Manila, that dominated shipping lanes. No important policy maker sought a mainland presence; 'McKinleyism' meant control of island bases near the continent of Asia.

The desire to spread liberal ideals, so easily pledged in 'taking up the white man's burden', sincerely moved many people. Those who believed that Asians must someday enter world affairs would risk expense to cultivate their allegiance. Tutelage would produce stability; self-government would come from guidance. The best of the liberal tradition would leaven the uncertain future. These spokesmen were over-confident and inexperienced, but not ignoble.

The Senate and press discussed constitutionality, world politics, and national purpose, but the public responded most to duty and prestige. The President distributed patronage, heard out and persuaded doubtful leaders, and cautiously· outlined a world role. On the evening of 5 February 1899, fighting unexpectedly broke out between Filipino insurgents and American troops in Manila. The Senate approved the treaty the following day with one vote to spare, testifying to McKinley's quiet but effective executive leadership.

The nation accepted the war's results, but Asia remained unfamiliar. Many Americans remembered Commodore Perry's opening of Japan, bought exotic imports, and contributed to Christian missions. Officials were more knowledgeable, and knew that a fresh policy must follow Philippine annexation, to deal with the larger question of China's destiny. The battle of Manila Bay came at a time when China seemed ready to collapse, creating dangerous tensions among European powers. Policy makers saw both a responsibility and an opportunity to help stabilize the situation and develop long-term influence. The administration did not seek a treaty port or sphere of influence, but used the Philippines to announce that the United States must figure in future arrangements.

China seemed to be the major future market for western products. McKinley was devoted to international tariff reciprocity, both to sell goods and to shape economic growth. Like other spokesmen, he depicted an ever-enlarging oriental market, which the United States could enter by cooperating with established Europeans. Enthusiasm, however, outran facts. Few of the alleged 400,000,000 customers lived within the reach of traders. No transportation system penetrated the vast backcountry, though foreign technicians operating through a stable Peking government could build one with outside capital. Western goods were not suited to oriental needs, except for kerosene and cheap textiles. Hatred of foreigners, which few people comprehended, was a formidable obstacle to bringing China into a world system based on western ideals. And however much they might want to buy, the Chinese were simply poor.

Yet sheer numbers were dazzling, the treaty ports were prosperous, and manufactured goods accounted for 90 percent of American trade with China in the mid Nineties. The volume of exports rose from $3,000,000 to $13,000,000, a rate that obscured the small base, and that promised indefinite returns if westerners provided credit and expertise. The Open Door Notes of 1899 and 1900 thus sought to guarantee reciprocal free trade within existing spheres of influence, and to maintain China's integrity and avoid a dangerous scramble for territory. Both Chinese and Europeans hopefully would welcome a moderating American influence, and the United States could avoid a potentially dangerous presence on the mainland. China was inevitably subordinate in the minds of foreign statesmen; she had not been united in recent times, and seemed permanently weak. By the time she attained genuine independence, her interests hopefully would coincide with the West's.

Unexpected events, not intent, undermined the policy. European power naturally impressed a generation, including colonials, who saw no reason to doubt that the sun would always set on British territory. Optimistic Americans saw a trend toward rational arbitration in the diplomatic arrangements that averted international crises over the Philippines, China, and the United States' sudden expansion. Other powers seemed ready to accord their new partner a moderating role. A steadily increasing standard of living, new communications, and an interdependent world made warfare among 'civilized' nations seem remote, if not unthinkable. Expansionist activity in the 1890s appeared to indicate a diversion of national tensions, and a willingness to compromise immediate desires for long-term stability that benefited everyone.

McKinley's foreign policy and maintenance of national unity increased his personal stature and presidential authority. He ideally symbolized the country's sense of enlarged purpose and the belief that a willingness to compromise divisive issues accompanied materialism in human affairs. He devoted the remainder of his term to organizing the dependencies and settling outstanding diplomatic problems. The army cooperated with civilian volunteers and politicians to begin reconstructing Cuba, and helped the new Republic established in 1902. Puerto Rico's future was less certain. But Hawaii became a territory, destined for ultimate statehood, which illustrated the

American system's flexibility. A volunteer army suppressed Filipino *insurrectos*, but the President quickly established civil rule. Most planners assumed the Islands would be independent someday. Britain accepted an enlarged American role both in the Caribbean and the world by acceding the right to build and fortify an isthmian canal.

The persistent desire to combine predictable growth and political liberalism, and the belief that well-being produced social harmony by enlarging personal security and property, seemed well-harmonized. Critics attacked 'McKinley imperialism', but the President won a handsome re-election in 1900. Yet he sought no more territory, an official attitude which persisted after his tragic assassination in 1901. Administrations watched Central America and the Caribbean, and sometimes influenced diplomacy in Asia. War and empire helped prove national vitality and cohesion, but America turned inward to a 'Progressive Movement'. The public returned to traditional aversion to the exercise of power, and approved limited force only to secure clearly defined goals in a familiar setting, as in Panama.

Dramatic events took the United States into world politics at a time when liberalism seemed to justify material goals. Expansionism's grandeur, and its combination of duty and possible long-term stability briefly captivated the American people. But the McKinley administration's policies were responsible, limited, and cautious. Officials did not overestimate either American power in the world arena, or domestic public support. They avoided full scale colonialism or active treaty cooperation with Europeans, and pragmatically sought a mediating middle course. No realistic alternative to this approach appeared. The nation could not remain outside world affairs; and it could not affect future developments without a formal presence, as in the Philippines.

In one large sense, public approval of expansionism reflected the nationalization of American life. Political cohesion, social stability, prosperity, and a sense of direction emerged from the brief crisis of the mid Nineties, and ended doubts about the ability to create a pluralistic society. And overseas expansion was not accidental or sudden. It came after at least a generation of discussion, amid technological and social changes that in effect brought world problems to the United States.

Special interest groups exerted pressure and sought defined goals, but expansionism appealed to the great majority of the people for larger reasons than immediate self-interest. Yet Americans sought influence rather than territory, presence more than power. Expansionism's appeals naturally faded as its risks and costs clarified in changing patterns of world power. Ironically enough the United States did not enforce harmony among world powers precisely because she did not embrace full-scale armament or adopt a permanent imperial role. But her experience was a natural, if not inevitable, part of the effort to combine idealism and self-interest in foreign policies that contemporaries thought were morally better than those of 'conservative' foreign powers.

Bibliographical Essay

A NUMBER of perceptive foreigners visited the United States in the late nineteenth century, and their accounts are valuable sources. Paul Bourget, a popular French society novelist, wrote *Outre-mer: Impressions of America* (London: T. Fisher, Unwin, 1895), which reports on manners, society, and regional differences. S. C. de Soissons, *A Parisian in America* (Boston: Estes and Lauriat, 1896), has useful comments on daily life.

The most famous English observer, James Bryce, produced *The American Commonwealth*, 2 vols. (New York: 1893–4). This study has influenced thinking about the United States on both sides of the Atlantic, but Bryce's observations are often debatable. His analyses of government in particular sometimes reflect an upper-class bias, rather than a deep understanding of the emerging party system. James Fullarton Muirhead toured the country in the 1890s, gathering information for the Baedeker guidebook firm, and incorporated many astute and appreciative observations in *America, The Land of Contrasts* (London: John Lane, 1898). George W. Steevens, foreign correspondent for the London *Daily Mail*, crossed the country during 1896, and offered local color and good political analysis in *The Land of the Dollar* (London: W. Blackwood, 1897). Professor David A. Shannon edited the journal of a famous Englishwoman, *Beatrice Webb's American Diary, 1898* (Madison: University of Wisconsin Press, 1963). Mrs Webb looked through both genteel and reformist spectacles, and said more about herself than the United States, but repeats a number of instructive anecdotes.

The Polish novelist Henry Sienkiewicz sent dispatches home during a tour in the 1870s, which Charles Morley collected in *Portrait of America: Letters of Henry Sienkiewicz* (New York: Columbia University Press, 1959). The German Hugo Munsterberg, who taught psychology at Harvard, was sympathetic in *The Americans* (New York: McClure, Phillips, 1904).

A number of general secondary works analyze the era. Harold

U. Faulkner, *Politics, Expansion and Reform* (New York: Harper, 1959), covers the 1890s from a somewhat dated viewpoint. Samuel P. Hays, *The Response to Industrialism, 1885–1914* (Chicago: University of Chicago Press, 1957), sparked fresh interest by taking the era and its issues seriously. Most subjects of public concern are covered in a new and enlarged edition of *The Gilded Age* (Syracuse: Syracuse University Press, 1970), edited by H. Wayne Morgan.

Biographies are a major source of information on politics and public policy. Harry Barnard, *Eagle Forgotten: The Life of John Peter Altgeld* (Indianapolis: Bobbs, Merrill, 1938), covers the career of Illinois' Democratic reform governor of the 1890s. Leland L. Sage, *William Boyd Allison* (Iowa City: State Historical Society of Iowa, 1956), deals with a major midwestern Republican senator with national influence. George F. Howe, *Chester A. Arthur* (New York: Dodd, Mead, 1934), is a useful presidential biography.

James G. Blaine, the era's most fascinating political figure, awaits an exhaustive study. A cousin of Blaine's, Gail Hamilton, wrote *Biography of James G. Blaine* (Norwich, Conn.: Henry Bill Pub. Co., 1895), which is now valuable chiefly for the personal correspondence it contains. David S. Muzzey, *James G. Blaine* (New York: Dodd, Mead, 1934), is the standard study.

Paolo E. Coletta has completed a three volume biography of William Jennings Bryan. Though the author's conclusions about politics in the 1890s are sometimes debatable, *William Jennings Bryan. I. Political Evangelist, 1860–1908* (Lincoln: University of Nebraska Press, 1964), is very useful.

The only Democratic president of the period has received considerable attention. Allan Nevins, *Grover Cleveland: A Study in Courage* (New York: Dodd, Mead, 1932), rests on original research but is too laudatory of Cleveland both as a personality and as a politician. The same author's *Letters of Grover Cleveland, 1850–1908* (Boston: Houghton, Mifflin, 1933), contains important correspondence. Horace S. Merrill analyzed Cleveland and the Democratic party in a brief, critical work, *Bourbon Leader: Grover Cleveland and the Democartic Party* (Boston: Houghton, Mifflin, 1957).

President Garfield was a contemporary hero who seemed to fulfill much of the American success story. Theodore Clarke Smith, *Life and Letters of James Abram Garfield*, 2 vols. (New Haven: Yale University Press, 1935), is a mine of information drawn from the Garfield papers. Robert G. Caldwell, *James A. Garfield, Party Chieftain* (New York: Dodd, Mead, 1931), is briefer.

Herbert Croly produced a sound, sympathetic biography, *Marcus Alonzo Hanna: His Life and Work* (New York: Macmillan, 1912). Benjamin Harrison is the subject of a three volume study by Harry J. Sievers. *Benjamin Harrison: Hoosier Statesman, 1865–1888* (New York: University Publishers, 1959), and *Benjamin Harrison: Hoosier President* (New York: Bobbs, Merrill, 1968), are useful for Harrison's personal life, but are often disappointing in dealing with politics. Harry J. Barnard helped rehabilitate the nineteenth president in *Rutherford B. Hayes and His America* (Indianapolis: Bobbs, Merrill, 1954).

President William McKinley's historical reputation has undergone some strange changes. Widely liked and respected during his lifetime, McKinley slipped into obscurity after 1901 because of a colorful successor and new national problems. It became stylish to see him as a weak, conservative president. Margaret Leech softened this erroneous view with *In the Days of McKinley* (New York: Harper, 1959), which focuses on family and social life, but contains a wealth of information on the administration. H. Wayne Morgan, *William McKinley and His America* (Syracuse: Syracuse University Press, 1963), is a full-scale biography, emphasizing McKinley's role as a moderate Republican who managed the chaotic party system with great skill.

Alexander Clarence Flick, *Samuel Jones Tilden* (New York: Dodd, Mead, 1939), is too favorable toward that laissez-faire Democrat, but is important for politics in the 1870s. Mark D. Hirsch studied a more robust politician and businessman in *William C. Whitney* (New York: Dodd, Mead, 1948), a biography which is basic to understanding the Democratic party in the 1880s and 1890s.

Some more general treatments of politics are important. Matthew Josephson, *The Politicos, 1865–1896* (New York: Harcourt, Brace, 1938), is chiefly responsible for the erroneous view that parties in the Gilded Age debated meaningless issues. H. Wayne Morgan, *From Hayes to McKinley: National Party Politics, 1877–1896* (Syracuse: Syracuse University Press, 1969), is the most recent comprehensive survey. Ari A. Hoogenboom, *Outlawing the Spoils* (Urbana: University of Illinois Press, 1961), questions the motives of Mugwump reformers, and sets the civil service question in the context of party development. J. Rogers Hollingsworth, *The Whirligig of Politics: The Democracy of Cleveland and Bryan* (Chicago: University of Chicago Press, 1963), criticizes the Cleveland

Democrats for adhering to old ideas in the 1890s. Though not primarily political, Geoffrey Blodgett, *The Gentle Reformers: Massachusetts Democrats in the Cleveland Era* (Cambridge: Harvard University Press, 1966), brilliantly depicts genteel groups facing social change.

A few regional studies are valuable for national affairs. C. Vann Woodward's *Origins of the New South, 1877–1913* (Baton Rouge: Louisiana State University Press, 1951), is the standard coverage of the South. Howard R. Lamar studied important western developments in *Dakota Territory, 1861–1889* (New Haven: Yale University Press, 1956), and *The Far Southwest, 1846–1912* (New Haven: Yale University Press, 1966). Lewis L. Gould, *Wyoming: A Political History, 1868–1896* (New Haven: Yale University Press, 1968), recounts how a local Republican party was built with patronage and national recognition. Robert R. Dykstra, *The Cattle Towns* (New York: Alfred Knopf, 1968), will hopefully help turn western history toward the problems of urban growth and politics. Gene M. Gressley, *Bankers and Cattlemen* (New York: Alfred Knopf, 1966), is important for showing how a regional economy responded to outside investors and new markets.

Agrarian interests that protested the force and variety of industrial change have received much historical attention. John D. Hicks, *The Populist Revolt* (Minneapolis: University of Minnesota Press, 1931), is the standard account of the Farmers' Alliance in politics. Robert F. Durden, *The Climax of Populism: The Election of 1896* (Lexington: University of Kentucky Press, 1965), unravels the Populist fusion campaigns of 1896, and assesses the movement's leadership and goals. The issue of *Agricultural History* for April 1965 contains essays by Professors Norman Pollack, Irwin Unger, Oscar Handlin, and J. Rogers Hollingsworth which offer a good cross-section of recent thinking about Populism.

There is a wealth of writing on economic policy, and the general reader might well begin with Sidney Fine, *Laissez-faire and the General Welfare State: A Study of Conflict in American Thought, 1865–1901* (Ann Arbor: University of Michigan Press, 1956). Edward C. Kirkland summarized an immense range of economic practice with insight and good sense in *Industry Comes of Age: Business, Labor and Public Policy, 1860–1897* (New York: Holt, Rinehart, and Winston, 1961), which also contains an excellent bibliographical guide. Two of the same author's books deal with the businessman's ideology: *Dream and Thought in the Business Community, 1860–1900*

(Ithaca: Cornell University Press, 1956); and *Business in the Gilded Age* (Madison: University of Wisconsin Press, 1952). Kirkland's comments in 'Economic Growth and Change: 1865–1890,' in John A. Garraty [ed.], *Interpreting American History: Conversations with Historians*, 2 vols. (New York: Macmillan, 1969), II, 3–19, are no less insightful for being informal. Louis M. Hacker offers a national viewpoint in *The World of Andrew Carnegie, 1865–1900* (Philadelphia: Lippincott, 1967).

The railroad question has generated much historical controversy. Lee Benson, *Merchants, Farmers and Railroads: Railroad Regulation and New York Politics, 1850–1887* (Cambridge: Harvard University Press, 1955), shows that merchants and shippers were influential in securing regulation. Gabriel Kolko, *Railroads and Regulation, 1877–1916* (Princeton: Princeton University Press, 1965), criticizes the businessman's desire for minimal federal regulation that allegedly promoted consolidation. The general trust problem is debated in Hans B. Thorelli, *The Federal Anti-Trust Policy* (Baltimore: Johns Hopkins Press, 1955); and in William Letwin, *Law and Economic Policy in America: The Evolution of the Sherman Antitrust Act* (New York: Random House, 1965).

The currency question was the era's most volatile economic issue in national politics. Robert P. Sharkey, *Money, Class and Party* (Baltimore: Johns Hopkins Press, 1959); and Irwin Unger, *The Greenback Era: A Social and Political History of American Finance, 1865–1879* (Princeton: Princeton University Press, 1964), destroyed many assumptions about interest groups that sought various kinds of currency and economic policies. Both authors show that support for gold, silver, or paper money depended on one's kind of business, location, moral viewpoint, and place in society. The same themes are extended in Walter T. K. Nugent, *Money and American Society, 1865–1880* (New York: Free Press, 1968), which also traces the efforts to secure an international bi-metallism agreement.

The second economic issue in politics, tariff protection, needs a full study. Protection's political appeals are obvious, and it was a major factor in party alignments. Its actual economic impact, however, remains unclear. Edward Stanwood, *American Tariff Controversies in the Nineteenth Century*, 2 vols. (Boston: Houghton, Mifflin, 1903), is protectionist and descriptive, but contains information and analysis historians have overlooked. A typical shallow attack on the tariff is Ida Tarbell, *The Tariff in Our Times* (New York: Macmillan, 1911). The standard scholarly account remains Frank W. Taussig, *The Tariff History of the United States*, 5th ed. (New York: Putnam's, 1910.)

A recent reassessment of America's world role has been at least partly responsible for new studies of Gilded Age diplomacy. David M. Pletcher, *The Awkward Years: Foreign Policy Under Garfield and Arthur* (Columbia, Mo.: University of Missouri Press, 1962), is broader than its subtitle indicates, and touches on inter-American developments, and the role of domestic politics in foreign policy.

William Appleman Williams has promoted an economic thesis, insisting in *The Tragedy of American Diplomacy* (New York: Delta Books, 1961, rev. ed.) that a search for overseas markets has motivated American foreign relations. In *The Roots of the Modern American Empire* (New York: Random House, 1970), Williams argues that the agrarian sector of society formulated the rationale for economic expansion, then convinced national politicians and businessmen of its merits. Walter La Feber used Latin America to test the Williams thesis in *The New Empire: An Interpretation of American Expansion, 1860–1898* (Ithaca: Cornell University Press, 1963). The theme was carried to the Orient in Thomas McCormick's *China Market* (Chicago: Quadrangle Books, 1967). These and other authors generally argue that interest in overseas markets reflected economic overproduction and unnecessarily involved the United States with imperial powers. The 'informal imperialism' that resulted from these economic drives allegedly made America the *bête-noire* of emerging nations. This viewpoint generally inflates the importance of businessmen in politics, and often rests on mis-readings of policy formation. Some men and interests did indeed seek to expand foreign markets, but this was not the prime force behind American diplomacy. Economic motives were clear in the McKinley administration's general policy toward China, but did not convince the American people of expansionism's virtues. The government responded more to events than to planning or special influence. As Paul S. Holbo points out in 'Economics, Expansion, and Emotion: An Emerging Foreign Policy,' in *The Gilded Age*, rev. ed. (Syracuse: Syracuse University Press, 1970), Congress and public opinion were generally indifferent or hostile toward tariff reciprocity, shipping subsidies, and commercial agreements, which were all necessary for any serious economic expansionism. Paul A. Varg is surprised, with hindsight, at how Americans overestimated both the potential China market, and the durability of European imperialism, in *The Making of a Myth: The United States and China*,

1897–1912 (East Lansing: Michigan State University Press, 1968).

The most stimulating recent review of the period's diplomatic problems is John A. S. Grenville and George Berkeley Young, *Politics, Strategy and American Diplomacy: Studies in Foreign Policy, 1873–1917* (New Haven: Yale University Press, 1966). In a series of pungent essays, the authors generally argue that strategic considerations, world events, and domestic politics influenced foreign policy more than economics or ideology. They criticize Cleveland and praise McKinley; they show that Henry Cabot Lodge was not a jingo; and disprove the myth that Theodore Roosevelt ordered Dewey to Manila Bay without authorization.

The origins and results of the Spanish-American War figure in many recent books, including several mentioned above. In *America's Road to Empire: The War With Spain and Overseas Expansion* (New York: John Wiley, 1965), H. Wayne Morgan holds that McKinley pursued a logical Cuban policy and did not capitulate to politicians or editors in April 1898. Lester D. Langley, *The Cuban Policy of the United States* (New York: John Wiley, 1968), is useful for reactions to both the Ten Years' War of 1868–78, and the insurrection of the 1890s. Ernest R. May, *Imperial Democracy* (New York: Harcourt, Brace, 1961), rests on multi-archival research, but May does not understand domestic power arrangements, and misjudges McKinley's personality and policy. Robert L. Beisner discussed the opposition to overseas expansion in *Twelve Against Empire: The Anti-Imperialists, 1898–1900* (New York: McGraw-Hill, 1968), which is chiefly intellectual history. Ernest R. May, *American Imperialism: A Speculative Essay* (New York: Atheneum, 1968), tries to show the influence of special groups in creating public support for expansion.

Two recent books have a good deal of insight into imperialism's origins and support. A. P. Thornton, *Doctrines of Imperialism* (New York: John Wiley and Sons, 1965), analyzes the formation of policy and reigning ideas. Heinz Gollwitzer, *Europe in the Age of Imperialism, 1880–1914* (New York: Harcourt, Brace, 1969), is brief, but offers some suggestive parallels to the American experience, and notes that imperialism was a product of liberal thought, with widespread appeal in nationalizing societies.

Urban history has attracted fresh concern in recent years. Blake McKelvey, *The Urbanization of America, 1860–1915* (New Brunswick: Rutgers University Press, 1963), is a general survey. Stanley Buder, *Pullman: An Experiment in Industrial Order and Community*

Planning, 1880–1930 (New York: Oxford University Press, 1967), re-examines the model town for George Pullman's workers near Chicago. Buder is sympathetic to Pullman's ideal of a healthful, pleasant town, but notes that paternalism did not fit human needs. Seymour Mandelbaum, *Boss Tweed's New York* (New York: John Wiley, 1965), shows how political organizations and 'bosses' met the material and emotional needs of constituents in the absence of formal institutions designed to help urban populations.

There are numerous histories of cities, of varying quality, but Bessie Louise Pierce, *A History of Chicago: Vol. III. The Rise of a Modern City, 1871–1893* (New York: Alfred Knopf, 1957), is an excellent study of urban problems, planning, and city life. Transportation systems had a great deal to do with housing patterns, industrial development, and population mobility, as Sam B. Warner shows in *Streetcar Suburbs: The Process of Growth in Boston, 1870–1900* (Cambridge: Harvard University Press, 1962). The consciousness of and reaction to poverty and bad housing in New York, with ramifications for other cities, is traced in Roy Lubove, *The Progressives and the Slums: Tenement House Reform in New York City, 1890–1917* (Pittsburgh: University of Pittsburgh Press, 1962).

Interest in immigration has complemented concern for urban history. Marcus Lee Hansen, *The Immigrants in American History* (Cambridge: Harvard University Press, 1940), was a pioneer work. Oscar Handlin has written several books about the interactions of established values and immigrants: *Race and Nationality in American Life* (Boston: Little, Brown, 1957), and *The Uprooted* (Boston: Little, Brown, 1951), are useful. Maldwyn A. Jones, *American Immigration* (Chicago: University of Chicago Press, 1960), is a good general survey.

The reaction of settled Americans to immigrants is difficult to determine, though generalizations abound. John Higham, *Strangers in the Land* (New Brunswick: Rutgers University Press, 1955); and Barbara Salomon, *Ancestors and Immigrants* (Cambridge: Harvard University Press, 1956), criticize that response. Thomas N. Brown, *Irish-American Nationalism, 1870–1890* (Philadelphia: Lippincott, 1966), has many astute observations on the Irish role in politics and society. Edward N. Saveth, *American Historians and European Immigrants, 1875–1925* (New York: Columbia University Press, 1948), is useful.

Labor historians have generally focused on strikes and dramatic public events, which distorts the workers' story. Robert V. Bruce,

1877: Year of Violence (Indianapolis: Bobbs, Merrill, 1959), how-
ever, is a brilliant re-creation of that year's railroad strikes. Donald
L. McMurry, *The Great Burlington Strike of 1888* (Cambridge:
Harvard University Press, 1956), covers both sides of the dispute.
Almont Lindsey, *The Pullman Strike* (Chicago: University of
Chicago Press, 1942), is a classic account, but is focused closely on
Chicago, while the strike had national ramifications. Henry David,
The History of the Haymarket Affair (New York: Russell and Russell
edition, 1958), remains the standard account of that famous
incident.

In a more general vein, John R. Commons, *et al*, *History of Labor
in the United States*, 4 vols. (New York: Macmillan, 1926–35), contains a great deal of information. Philip Taft has written three basic
books: *Organized Labor in American History* (New York: Harper,
1964); *The AFL in the Time of Gompers* (New York: Harper, 1957);
and *The AFL From the Death of Gompers to the Merger* (New York:
Harper, 1959). An older study, Norman J. Ware, *The Labor
Movement in the United States, 1860–1895* (New York: D. Appleton,
1925), remains informative.

Some of the reasons for American labor's dislike of doctrine are
explained in Gerald N. Grob, *Workers and Utopia* (Evanston:
Northwestern University Press, 1961). Herbert J. Gutman, 'The
Workers' Search for Power,' in *The Gilded Age*, rev. ed. (Syracuse:
Syracuse University Press, 1970), shows how workers in small
towns differed from those in large cities.

Education was a major aspect of nationalization, but has only
recently begun to receive the scholarly attention it merits. Studies
of state and local responses to educational changes and needs are
scarce, but Russell Thomas, *The Search for a Common Learning:
General Education, 1800–1960* (New York: McGraw-Hill, 1962), is
a good interpretation. Laurence R. Veysey, *The Emergence of the
American University* (Chicago: University of Chicago Press, 1965),
is an outstanding book that charts the conflicting theories and
social reactions in the rise of higher learning after 1865. Richard J.
Storr, *The Beginnings of Graduate Education in America* (Chicago:
University of Chicago Press, 1953); and Juergen Herbst, *The
German Historical School in American Scholarship* (Ithaca: Cornell
University, 1965), are both important for academic specialization
and the transfer of foreign ideas and techniques.

Histories of individual universities tend to be discursive, but a
few analyze general problems. Morris Bishop, *A History of Cornell*

(Ithaca: Cornell University Press, 1962), is sound. Hugh Hawkins, *Pioneer: A History of The Johns Hopkins University, 1874–1889* (Ithaca: Cornell University Press, 1960), is an excellent work. Richard J. Storr, *Harper's University* (Chicago: University of Chicago Press, 1964), recounts the establishment of the University of Chicago in the mid 1890s, and is especially good on faculty recruitment, fund-raising, and community response.

Rayford W. Logan studied a leading Negro university in *Howard University: The First Hundred Years* (New York: New York University Press, 1969). Two Midwestern universities that shared common experiences while expanding services and ideals are dealt with in Robert N. Manley, *Frontier University, 1869–1919* (Lincoln: University of Nebraska Press, 1969); and in Winton U. Solberg's able work, *The University of Illinois, 1867–1894: An Intellectual and Cultural History* (Urbana: University of Illinois Press, 1968).

Popular culture has not received its scholarly due, largely because patterns of development and sources are difficult to organize. Robert D. Cross offers important generalizations about the era's values and tastes in 'American Society, 1865–1914,' in Garraty, *Interpreting American History*, II, 23–42. Russell Lynes, *The Tastemakers* (New York: Harper, 1954), is an interesting though not profound over-view. Sports reflected a good deal of popular taste and attitudes, and John Rickards Betts, 'The Technological Revolution and the Rise of Sports, 1850–1900,' *Mississippi Valley Historical Review*, 40 (September 1953), 231–56, has many good observations. Allison Danzig, *The History of American Football* (New York: Macmillan, 1955); and David Quentin Voight, *American Baseball: From Gentleman's Sport to the Commissioner System* (Norman: University of Oklahoma Press, 1966), 1966), are both useful.

The Chautauqua movement deserves a full-study, which would reveal a great deal about the impact of industrialism on older values. Joseph E. Gould, *The Chautauqua Movement* (New York: State University of New York Press, 1961), is a perceptive, but unfortunately brief account. Victoria Case, *We Called it Culture* (New York: Doubleday, 1948), is an important memoir.

The artifacts of daily life are analyzed in *Made in America* (New York: Doubleday, 1948), by John A. Kouwenhoven, who discovers a great deal of esthetic merit and functionalism in American tools, implements, and machinery. Siegfried Giedion's fascinating work, *Mechanization Takes Command* (New York: Oxford University

Press, 1946), analyzes the impact of machine goods, standardization, and technical sophistication on daily life.

The sources on American literature are abundant. Jay C. Martin, *Harvests of Change: American Literature, 1865–1914* (New York: Prentice, Hall, 1967), combines literary criticism and cultural history, and is especially important for regional figures. Werner Berthoff, *The Ferment of Realism: American Literature, 1884–1919* (New York: The Free Press, 1966), is a good assessment of the main aspects of Realism and Naturalism. Larzer Ziff discusses some of the reasons why the new critical spirit evident among writers failed to mature in *The American 1890s: The Life and Times of a Lost Generation* (New York: Viking, 1966).

Justin Kaplan, *Mr. Clemens and Mark Twain* (New York: Simon and Schuster, 1966), is a brilliant analysis of Clemens's personality and work. Louis J. Budd, *Mark Twain: Social Philosopher* (Bloomington: Indiana University Press, 1962), is an engaging account of Clemens's social writings. William Dean Howells is the subject of a two volume biography by Edwin Cady, *The Road to Realism* (Syracuse: Syracuse University Press, 1956), and *The Realist at War* (Syracuse: Syracuse University Press, 1958). Clara Marburg Kirk, *W. D. Howells and Art in His Time* (New Brunswick: Rutgers University Press, 1965), has some significant material on Howells as an art critic. The major spokesman of local color is treated sympathetically in Jean Holloway, *Hamlin Garland* (Austin: University of Texas Press, 1960). The literature on Henry James is voluminous, but Leon Edel's multi-volume biography is a good starting place.

The present study has not touched upon intellectual history, and the interested reader could begin with Henry Steele Commager, *The American Mind* (New Haven: Yale University Press, 1950). Ralph H. Gabriel, *The Course of American Democratic Thought* (New York: Ronald Press, 1940), is important, as is Morton G. White, *Social Thought in America: The Revolt Against Formalism* (New York: Viking Press, 1949). Paul F. Boller, Jr, *American Thought in Transition: The Impact of Evolutionary Naturalism, 1865–1900* (New York: Rand, McNally, 1969), is a good recent synthesis, with a full bibliographical guide.

Black history is justly receiving fresh attention. Two well-established reviews, *The Journal of Negro History*, and *The Negro History Bulletin*, contain many important articles. John Hope Franklin, *From Slavery to Freedom: A History of Negro Americans*, 3rd ed. (New York: Knopf, 1967), is the standard survey. *The Making of Black America, Vol. II. The Black Community in Modern America* (New York: Atheneum, 1969), edited by August Meier and Elliott Rudwick, reprints a cross-section of scholarly writings. Rayford W. Logan, *The Negro in American Life and Thought: The Nadir, 1877–1901* (New York: Dial Press, 1954), is the standard account for the period. August Meier has covered Negro thought and reaction to national events in *Negro Thought in America, 1880–1915* (Ann Arbor: University of Michigan Press, 1963), which is especially useful for studying black businessmen, editors, and professionals.

Fragmentary records complicate the historian's efforts to chart Negro urban life, but three recent studies are helpful: Seth M. Scheiner, *Negro Mecca: A History of the Negro in New York City, 1865–1920* (New York: New York University Press, 1965); Gilbert Osofsky, *Harlem: The Making of a Ghetto* (New York: Harper, 1966); and Allan H. Spear, *Black Chicago: The Making of a Negro Ghetto, 1890–1920* (Chicago: University of Chicago Press, 1967).

Numerous studies of the South deal with the Negro, but C. Vann Woodward, *The Strange Career of Jim Crow*, rev. ed. (New York: Oxford University Press, 1966), is a basic interpretation of segregation, though some scholars have challenged its conclusions. Vernon Lane Wharton, *The Negro in Mississippi, 1865–1890* (Chapel Hill: University of North Carolina Press, 1947), is a pioneer work of great merit.

Books on American music abound, but few discuss the total cultural setting. General surveys include: Gilbert Chase, *America's Music: From the Pilgrims to the Present* (New York: McGraw-Hill, 1955); John Tasker Howard, *Our American Music*, 4th ed. (New York: Thomas Crowell, 1965), which though dull is useful for the era's composers; Wilfrid Mellers, *Music in a New Found Land* (London: Barrie and Rockcliff, 1964), which is good on Charles Ives, the composer whose work post-dates the period in question; and Irving Sablosky, *American Music* (Chicago: University of Chicago Press, 1969).

The most famous American composer of the era awaits a full biography. Edward MacDowell's own writings are in *Critical and Historical Essays* (Boston: Arthur P. Schmidt Co., 1912). Two old studies are the chief secondary source for his life and work: Lawrence Gilman, *Edward MacDowell: A Study* (New York: John Lane Co., 1908); and Elizabeth F. Page, *Edward MacDowell: His*

Work and Ideals (New York: Dodge Pub. Co., 1910). Neil Leonard has written an important article, 'Edward MacDowell and the Realists,' *American Quarterly*, 28 (Summer 1966), 175–82.

Most of the books on symphony orchestras are shallow, but John H. Mueller, *The American Symphony Orchestra: A Social History of Musical Taste* (Bloomington: Indiana University Press, 1951), is a distinguished monograph that tries to chart the development of audience taste.

The economic and social importance of operatic production is seldom analyzed in the numerous works on the subject, which usually merely discuss glamorous personalities. Irving Kolodin, *The Story of the Metropolitan Opera, 1883–1966* (New York: Alfred Knopf, 1966), however, contains useful information. Ronald L. Davis, *Opera in Chicago* (New York: Appleton, Century, 1966), is chatty, but has some insight into the workings of New York's chief operatic rival. Two biographies of singers give a good view of musical life: Ira Glackens, *Yankee Diva: Lillian Nordica and the Golden Days of Opera* (New York: Coleridge Press, 1963); and Joseph Wechsberg, *Red Plush and Black Velvet: The Story of Melba and Her Times* (Boston: Little, Brown, 1961).

American painting offers a great variety of subjects for study. Two recent books give background for post-Civil War developments. Lillian B. Miller, *Patrons and Patriotism: The Encouragement of the Fine Arts in the United States, 1790–1860* (Chicago: University of Chicago Press, 1966), details the story of artists in search of public support and recognition. Neil Harris, *The Artist in American Society: The Formative Years, 1790–1860* (New York: George Braziller, 1968), is concerned with public attitudes toward the arts, painters' views of themselves, and debate over artistic ideals.

Three contemporary esthetic statements are important: John La Farge, *Considerations on Painting* (New York: Macmillan Co., 1895), is significant both for La Farge's work, and for world influences on American artists. Kenyon Cox, *The Classic Point of View: Six Lectures on Painting* (New York: Scribner's, 1911), summarizes the resistance to 'modernism.' Willard Huntington Wright, *Modern Painting* (New York: John Lane, 1915), discusses things to come.

A few minor painters left good accounts of the art life. Cecilia Beaux, who gained some stature as a portraitist, wrote *Background With Figures* (Boston: Houghton, Mifflin, 1930). Will H. Low produced two discursive volumes that delineate the impact of

foreign study and travel on Americans: *A Chronicle of Friendships*
(New York: Scribner's, 1908), and *A Painter's Progress* (New York:
Scribner's, 1910). *Some Went This Way* (Chicago: privately
printed, 1945), by a prominent illustrator, Ralph Fletcher Seymour, captures the tone of the revolution in printing and illustrat-
ing. Elihu Vedder, *The Digressions of V* (Boston: Houghton,
Mifflin, 1910), is the rambling recollections of a painter of exotic
and mystical subjects.

Several well-produced contemporary histories attest to public
interest in painting, and remain important sources of both
information and critical attitudes. Sadakichi Hartmann, *A History
of American Art*, 2 vols. (Boston: L. C. Page, 1902), is readable and
generally sympathetic toward innovations. Samuel Isham, *The
History of American Painting* (New York: Macmillan, 1905), is more
traditionalist. Charles Henry Caffin, *The Story of American Painting*
(New York: Frederick A. Stokes, 1907), is good for minor figures.
Frank Jewett Mather, Jr, *Modern Painting: A Study of Tendencies*
(New York: Henry Holt, 1927), is an influential critic's magisterial
survey of western art. While Mather often misjudged 'moderns',
his general comments are applicable to the American scene. As in
most eras, critics were behind painters in accepting new subject-
matter and esthetic ideas, and were very conscious of established
standards.

Some later surveys are useful. Oliver W. Larkin, *Art and Life in
America*, rev. ed. (New York: Holt, Rinehart, Winston, 1960), is a
general account that often slights the Gilded Age. Eugen Neuhaus,
The History and Ideals of American Art (Palo Alto: Stanford Uni-
versity Press, 1931), is informed and insightful about many
painters. James Thomas Flexner, *That Wilder Image: The Painting
of America's Native School from Thomas Cole to Winslow Homer*
(Boston: Little, Brown, 1962), is dull but useful. Alfred V.
Frankenstein, *After the Hunt: William Harnett and Other American
Still Life Painters, 1870–1900* (Berkeley: University of California
Press, 1953), discusses the *coup-d'oeil* still life painters.

Two recent studies are stimulating. John W. McCoubrey,
American Tradition in Painting (New York: George Braziller, 1963),
is a brief analysis of the impact of space, natural grandeur, and
loneliness on American art. Barbara Novak, *American Painting of
the Nineteenth Century* (New York: Praeger, 1969), has some suggestive insights on American Impressionism and cosmopolitanism.

There is no full study of that cosmopolitanism, but several

works deal with foreign ideas in American art. David H. Dickason, *The Daring Young Men: The Story of the American Pre-Raphaelites* (Bloomington: Indiana University Press, 1953); and Roger B. Stein, *John Ruskin and Aesthetic Thought in America, 1840–1900* (Cambridge: Harvard University Press, 1967), discuss English influences. Hugh Honour, *Chinoiserie: The Vision of Cathay* (London: J. Murray, 1961); Clay Lancaster, *The Japanese Influence in America* (New York: Walton H. Rawls, 1963); and Lawrence W. Chisolm, *Fenollosa: The Far East and American Culture* (New Haven: Yale University Press, 1963), are all basic for understanding oriental influences.

Most of the period's painters deserve new treatments, but the following biographies are worth consulting: Edward V. Lucas, *Edwin Austin Abbey*, 2 vols. (New York: Scribner's, 1921), tells the story of a famous illustrator. Frederick A. Sweet, *Miss Mary Cassatt: Impressionist From Pennsylvania* (Norman: University of Oklahoma Press, 1966), is important for personal material. Katherine M. Roof, *The Life and Art of William Merritt Chase* (New York: Scribner's, 1917), is dated, but remains the only lengthy work on an influential and underestimated painter. The same is true of Norbert Heerman, *Frank Duveneck* (Boston: Houghton, Mifflin, 1918).

Thomas Eakins has gained a good deal of historical attention. The standard life is Lloyd Goodrich, *Thomas Eakins* (New York: Whitney Museum, 1933); but Sylvan Schendler, *Eakins* (Boston: Little, Brown, 1967), is also important. Robert Henri's work postdates the period in hand, but his views are in *The Art Spirit* (Philadelphia: Lippincott, 1923), drawn from lectures and interviews. His school is depicted in an outstanding new study, William Inness Homer, *Robert Henri and His Circle* (Ithaca: Cornell University Press, 1969).

There are many books of varying quality about Winslow Homer, and Lloyd Goodrich, *Winslow Homer* (New York: Whitney Museum, 1944), is a sound introduction. Philip C. Beam, *Winslow Homer at Prout's Neck* (Boston: Little, Brown, 1966), is largely biographical. Albert Ten Eyck Gardner, *Winslow Homer: American Artist, His World and His Work* (New York: Bramhall House, 1961), surveys both Homer's life and paintings.

William Morris Hunt merits a full-scale biography. Helen Knowlton, *Art-Life of William Morris Hunt* (Boston: Little, Brown, 1899), is thin and old fashioned, but contains useful contemporary material. Her two volumes of Hunt's *Talks on Art* (1875), (1883), and Henry Clay Angell, *Records of William M. Hunt* (Boston: J. R. Osgood Co., 1881), reveal Hunt's dynamic, fascinating personality.

There is no adequate biography of Sargent. Charles Merrill Mount, *John Singer Sargent* (New York: Norton, 1955), is tedious, overly long, and too narrowly focused on his personal life. Two older books remain valuable: William Howe Downes, *John S. Sargent* (Boston: Little, Brown, 1925), and Evan Charteris, *John Sargent* (New York: Scribner's, 1927). Two recent works, however, indicate growing interest in Sargent. The text of Richard Ormond, *John Singer Sargent: Paintings, Drawings, Watercolors* (New York: Harper & Row, 1970), is brief, but its illustrations are a good cross-section of Sargent's major painting styles. Ormond does not reproduce much of the famous murals, which merit a separate study. Donelson F. Hoopes, *Sargent Watercolors* (Cincinnati: Watson, Guptil, 1970), is an excellent introduction to the great portraitist's work in a dry medium.

American impressionism deserves attention both for its esthetic content and cultural significance. There are a few useful catalogues of the works of individual painters. Dorothy Weir Young, *The Life and Letters of J. Alden Weir* (New Haven: Yale University Press, 1960), treats a major impressionist, and has valuable material on the importance of European training and travel to American students, and on the reception of Impressionist work in the United States.

Though Whistler was not technically an 'American' painter, his personality and work are irresistible. An authorized biography by two friends, Elizabeth and Joseph Pennell, *The Life of James McNeill Whistler*, 2 vols. (Philadelphia: Lippincott, 1908), remains standard despite lapses of both fact and judgement. James Laver, *Whistler*, 2nd ed. (London: Faber and Faber, 1951), is a brief, balanced account. Whistler's works are emphasized in three excellent volumes: Denys Sutton, *Nocturne: The Art of James McNeill Whistler* (Philadelphia: Lippincott, 1964); the same author's *James McNeill Whistler: Paintings, Drawings, Etchings, and Watercolors* (London: Phaidon Books, 1966); and Donald Holden, *Whistler Landscapes and Seascapes* (New York: Watson, Guptil, 1969).

Mural painting attained unprecedented importance in the Gilded Age, but few scholars have assessed its esthetic value, or the reasons for its rise and decline. Edwin Howland Blashfield, a leading muralist, wrote *Mural Painting in America* (New York: Scribner's, 1913), which contains information on art life in general. Pauline King, *American Mural Painting* (Boston: Noyes, Platt, 1902), has important illustrations.

Eliot C. Clark, *History of the National Academy of Design, 1825–1953* (New York: Columbia University Press, 1954), is the standard treatment. Walter Pach, *The Art Museum in America* (New York: Pantheon Books, 1948), is an over-view of the museum movement. Other useful studies include: Neil Harris, 'The Gilded Age Revisited: Boston and the Museum Movement,' *American Quarterly*, 14 (Winter 1962), 545–66; Walter Muir Whitehill, *Museum of Fine Arts, Boston: A Centennial History*, 2 vols. (Cambridge: Harvard University Press, 1970); and Leo Lehrman, *The Museum: 100 Years and the Metropolitan Museum of Art* (New York: Viking, 1969).

Mrs Louisine Havemeyer wrote a delightful and perceptive memoir of her travels while collecting art, in *Sixteen to Sixty: Memoirs of a Collector* (New York: privately printed, 1961). Aline Saarinen, *The Proud Possessors* (New York: Random House, 1958), is a general survey of American collectors. Louise Hall Tharp's study of an engaging eccentric, *Mrs Jack: A Biography of Isabella Stewart Gardner* (Boston: Little, Brown, 1965), is important for Mrs Gardner's collection, and for assessing the era's taste.

Sculpture has not provoked as much scholarly interest as painting. Albert Ten Eyck Gardner, *Yankee Stonecutters: The First American School of Sculpture, 1800–1850* (New York: Metropolitan Museum, 1945), is important. Lorado Taft, *The History of American Sculpture* (New York: Macmillan, 1903), is a good contemporary work by a prominent sculptor. Wayne Craven, *Sculpture in America* (New York: Crowell, 1968), is an outstanding general survey.

James M. Dennis, *Karl Bitter: Architectural Sculptor, 1867–1915* (Madison: University of Wisconsin Press, 1967), is the well illustrated story of an important *beaux-arts* sculptor. Margaret Cresson, *Journey Into Fame: The Life of Daniel Chester French* (Cambridge: Harvard University Press, 1947), is standard. David H. Wallace, *John Rogers: The People's Sculptor* (Middletown, Conn.: Wesleyan University Press, 1967), is good for both Roger's work and public taste. Augustus Saint-Gaudens, *Reminiscences*, 2 vols. (New York: The Century Co., 1913), is a primary source. Louise Hall Tharp, *Saint-Gaudens and the Gilded Era* (Boston: Little, Brown, 1969), is almost entirely personal, and Saint-Gaudens' work deserves a full critical study.

Two collections of contemporary criticism on architecture are important for understanding building during the Gilded Age. Montgomery Schuyler, *American Architecture and Other Writings* (New York: Atheneum, 1964), is especially good for reaction to the Queen Anne style, the skyscraper, and the work of H. H. Richardson. William A. Coles [ed.], *Architecture and Society: Selected Essays of Henry Van Brunt* (Cambridge: Harvard University Press, 1969), contains good discussions of the *beaux-arts* style.

Carl Condit has written several important works on building technology, and the 'Chicago style', including: *American Building Art: The Nineteenth Century* (New York: Oxford University Press, 1960); *The Chicago School of Architecture* (Chicago: University of Chicago Press, 1964); and *The Rise of the Skyscraper* (Chicago: University of Chicago Press, 1952).

Many architects deserve new biographies. Charles Moore, *Daniel H. Burnham, Architect, Planner of Cities* (Boston: Houghton, Mifflin, 1921), is dated, but contains personal correspondence. The same is true of that author's *The Life and Times of Charles Follen McKim* (Boston: Houghton, Mifflin, 1929). Charles C. Baldwin, *Stanford White* (New York: Dodd, Mead, 1931), is thin, and the firm of McKim, Mead and White deserves a full, sympathetic study.

Henry H. Richardson attained respect and fame, but in retrospect, his style seems less successful than contemporaries thought. Nevertheless, two works are important for Richardson and architecture in general: Henry-Russell Hitchcock, *The Architecture of H. H. Richardson and His Times* (New York: Museum of Modern Art, 1936); and a glowing contemporary account lately reprinted, Mariana Griswold van Rensselaer, *Henry Hobson Richardson and His Work* (New York: Dover, 1969).

Louis Sullivan suffered the opposite fate – relative neglect while alive and indiscriminate praise from historians. Two books contain his lectures, observations, and memoirs: *The Autobiography of an Idea* (New York: American Institute of Architects, 1924); and *Kindergarten Chats* (New York: Wittenborn, Schultz, 1947). Three biographies cover his life and work: Albert Bush-Brown, *Louis Sullivan* (New York: Braziller, 1960); Paul Sherman, *Louis Sullivan: An Architect in American Thought* (New York: Prentice, Hall, 1962); and John Szarkowski, *The Idea of Louis Sullivan* (Minneapolis: University of Minnesota Press, 1956).

Concern for city planning was one of the many merits of the

era's architects. Julius G. Fabos, *et al*, *Frederick Law Olmstead, Sr.: Founder of Landscape Architecture in America* (Amherst: University of Massachusetts Press, 1968), has good illustrations and a sound text. John W. Reps, *The Making of Urban America: A History of City Planning in the United States* (Princeton: Princeton University Press, 1965), deals chiefly with the pre-Civil War period, but is useful for charting the elaborate *fin-de-siècle* plans to reshape major cities such as Chicago and Washington. Mel Scott, *American City Planning Since 1890* (Berkeley: University of California Press, 1969), carries the story forward. Vincent Scully recently contributed an often irascible, but delightful and perceptive over-view, *American Architecture and Urbanism* (New York: Praeger, 1969).

Notes

CHAPTER ONE

An Industrial Society

1. Quoted in Edward C. Kirkland, *Industry Comes of Age: Business, Labor and Public Policy, 1860–1897* (New York: Holt, Rinehart and Winston, 1961), 175.
2. Hugo Munsterberg, *The Americans* (New York: McClure, Phillips, 1904), 269.
3. Raymond B. Nixon, *Henry W. Grady* (New York: Alfred Knopf, 1943). 16–17, 90–92.
4. Henry James, *The American Scene* (New York: Harper Bros., 1907), 379.
5. *Commercial and Financial Chronicle*, 17 (6 June, 1885), 606–7.
6. Quoted in William Letwin, *Law and Economic Policy in America: The Evolution of the Sherman Anti-Trust Act* (New York: Random House, 1965), 55–6.
7. Henry Seidel Canby, *The Age of Confidence: Life in the Nineties* (New York: Farrar and Rinehart, 1934), 238.
8. Quoted in Kirkland, *Industry Comes of Age*, 395.
9. *Congressional Record*, 51st Congress, 1st Session, 2457ff.
10. Canby, *The Age of Confidence*, 25; see also John A. Garraty, *The New Commonwealth, 1877–1890* (New York: Harper and Row, 1968), esp. 78–178, for more information and an often differing view.
11. Kirkland, *Industry Comes of Age*, 345.
12. James Fullarton Muirhead, *America: The Land of Contrasts* (New York: John Lane Co., 1898), 275.
13. For more information on these attitudes, see Gerald N. Grob, *Workers and Utopia* (Evanston, Ill.: Northwestern University Press, 1961). Herbert G. Gutman, 'The Workers' Search for Power', in H. Wayne Morgan [ed.], *The Gilded Age* (Syracuse: Syracuse University Press, revised edition, 1970), is also important.

14. Quoted in Kirkland, *Industry Comes of Age*, 402.
15. Garraty, *The New Commonwealth*, 142.
16. Charles Morley [ed.], *Portrait of America: Letters of Henry Sienkiewiecz* (New York: Columbia University Press, 1959), 277.
17. James, *The American Scene*, 123–4; see also, Timothy Smith, 'Immigrant Social Attitudes and American Education, 1880–1930', *American Quarterly*, 21 (Fall 1969), 523–43.
18. Quoted in Louis M. Hacker, *The World of Andrew Carnegie, 1865–1901* (Philadelphia: J. B. Lippincott, 1968), 331.
19. Montgomery Schuyler, *American Architecture and Other Writings* (New York: Atheneum, 1964), 180; Carl Condit, *The Rise of the Skyscraper* (Chicago: University of Chicago Press, 1952), 18–19.
20. ibid., 75.
21. See James M. Dennis, *Karl Bitter: Architectural Sculptor, 1867–1915* (Madison: University of Wisconsin Press, 1967), 225ff.
22. Schuyler, *American Architecture*, 57.
23. ibid., 249, 261.
24. These and many other changes in daily living are discussed and analyzed in Siegried Giedion's fascinating book, *Mechanization Takes Command* (New York: Oxford University Press, 1948), 512–626.
25. ibid., 287–9.
26. Helen Campbell, 'Household Furnishings', *Architectural Record*, 6 (October–December 1896), 97–104.
27. See Robert Koch, *Louis C. Tiffany, Rebel in Glass* (New York: Crown Publishers, 1966).
28. See David H. Wallace, *John Rogers, The People's Sculptor* (Middletown, Conn.: Wesleyan University Press, 1967).
29. *The American Heritage History of Antiques From the Civil War to World War I* (New York: American Heritage, 1969), 88–91, well illustrates some of this fascinating material, and is a valuable work for the era's popular taste.
30. Siegfried Giedion, *Space, Time and Architecture* (Cambridge: Harvard University Press, 1941), 263–4.
31. The saltine's engaging saga is recounted in Lewis Atherton, *Main Street on the Middle Border* (Bloomington: Indiana University Press, 1954), 226–8.
32. Morley [ed.], *Portrait of America*, 9–10.
33. Kirkland, *Industry Comes of Age*, 273.

34. Atherton, *Main Street on the Middle Border*, 192–3; Joy J. Jackson, *New Orleans in the Gilded Age* (Baton Rouge: Louisiana State University Press, 1969), 263ff; Philip D. Jordan, *Ohio Comes of Age, 1873–1900* (Columbus: Ohio Historical Society, 1943), 353–6.

35. John R. Betts, 'The Technological Revolution and the Rise of Sports, 1850–1900', *Mississippi Valley Historical Review*, 40 (September, 1953), 213–56, is an important article.

36. Quoted in Howard Peckham, *The Making of The University of Michigan, 1817–1967* (Ann Arbor: University of Michigan Press, 1967), 77.

37. Kirkland, *Industry Comes of Age*, 341.

38. Walter P. Rogers, *Andrew D. White and the Modern University* (Ithaca: Cornell University Press, 1942), 6.

39. See Samuel Eliot Morison, *Three Centuries of Harvard, 1636–1936* (Cambridge: Harvard University Press, 1936), 326–7.

40. Hugh Hawkins, *Pioneer: A History of Johns Hopkins University, 1874–1889* (Ithaca: Cornell University Press, 1959), 68.

41. See Juergen Herbst, *The German Historical School in American Scholarship* (Ithaca: Cornell University Press, 1965), 31.

42. Quoted in Laurence R. Veysey, *The Emergence of the American University* (Chicago: University of Chicago Press, 1965), 296.

43. Frederick Rudolph, *The American College and University: A History* (New York: Alfred Knopf, 1962), 326–7.

44. Veysey, *The Emergence of the American University*, 266–7.

45. Munsterberg, *The Americans*, 392.

CHAPTER TWO

The Politics of Nationalism

1. *Harper's Weekly*, 21 (19 May, 1877), 382.

2. See James M. McPherson, 'Coercion or Conciliation: Abolitionists Debate President Hayes' Southern Policy', *New England Quarterly*, 39 (December 1966), 486.

3. Sherman to Robert O. Herbert, 19 June 1879, John Sherman papers, Library of Congress.

4. Charles Morley [ed.], *Portrait of America: Letters of Henry Sienkiewiecz* (New York: Columbia University Press, 1959), 94–5.

5. Roy P. Basler [ed.], *Collected Works of Abraham Lincoln*, 9 vols.

(New Brunswick, N.J.: Rutgers University Press, 1953), IV, 438.

6. Theodore Roosevelt, *Autobiography* (New York: Charles Scribner's Sons, 1926), 313–20.

7. Hayes to B. A. Hayes, 23 January 1873, Hayes papers.

8. See H. Wayne Morgan, 'William McKinley and the Tariff', *Ohio History*, 74 (Autumn 1965), 215–31.

9. Morison to David A. Wells, 7 September 1884, David A. Wells papers, Library of Congress.

10. Arthur Krock [ed.], *Editorials of Henry Watterson* (New York: Doubleday, Doran, 1923), 50.

11. Smith to Hayes, 9 July 1878, William Henry Smith papers, Ohio Historical Society, Columbus.

12. Wilson Vance to Schurz, 24 March 1878, Carl Schurz papers, Library of Congress.

13. *Commercial and Financial Chronicle*, 28 (4 January 1879), 1.

14. Frye to Wharton Barker, 4 December 1894, Wharton Barker papers, Library of Congress.

15. W. M. Dickson to W. K. Rogers, 25 March 1878, Hayes papers.

16. Diary of Rutherford B. Hayes, 22 April 1877, ibid.

17. Garfield to Blaine, 29 June 1880, James A. Garfield papers, Library of Congress.

18. Paul P. Van Riper, *History of the United States Civil Service* (Evanston, Ill.: Row, Peterson Co., 1958), 111–12.

19. Hayes to R. M. Hatfield, 22 March 1889, Hayes papers.

20. Shelby M. Cullom, *Fifty Years of Public Service* (Chicago: A. C. McClurg Co., 1911), 221.

21. Charles Hedges [ed.], *The Speeches of Benjamin Harrison* (New York: Lovell, Coryell and Co., 1892), 9–24.

22. Harrison to Whitelaw Reid, 27 September 1888, Benjamin Harrison papers, Library of Congress.

23. Leon Burr Richardson, *William E. Chandler, Republican* (New York: Dodd, Mead and Co., 1940), 412.

24. Sherman to L. J. Gartrell, 26 July 1890, Sherman papers.

25. L. T. Hunt to Sherman, 6 January 1891, ibid.

26. C. T. Russell, Jr, [ed.], *Speeches and Address of William E. Russell* (Boston: Little, Brown Co., 1894), 226.

27. Bayard to Don M. Dickinson, 11 July 1891, Don M. Dickinson papers, Library of Congress.

28. W. L. Wilson and T. B. Reed, 'The Issues of the Coming

Elections', *North American Review*, 159 (October 1894), 385–94.

29. Benjamin Harrison, *Views of an Ex-President* (Indianapolis: Bowen, Merrill Co., 1901), 384.

CHAPTER THREE

The Search for a National Culture

1. Charles H. Caffin, *The Story of American Painting* (New York: Frederick A. Stokes Co., 1907), 121.
2. Henry T. Tuckerman, *Book of the Artists* (New York: Putnam's, 1867), 28.
3. *Criticism and Fiction* (New York: Harper Bros., 1891), 41.
4. ibid., 46.
5. *A Connecticut Yankee in King Arthur's Court* (New York: Harper Bros., 1909), 285.
6. William Dean Howells, *My Mark Twain* (New York: Harper Bros., 1910), 108.
7. ibid., 100–1.
8. ibid., 49.
9. William Dean Howells, *A Hazard of New Fortunes* (New York: E. P. Dutton Co., 1952), 254.
10. Donald Pizer [ed.], *Hamlin Garland's Diaries* (San Marino, California: Huntington Library, 1968), 129.
11. Both quotations from Hamlin Garland, *Crumbling Idols* (Chicago: Stone and Kimball Co., 1894), 51, 57, 176.
12. Henry Blake Fuller, *Under the Skylights* (New York: D. Appleton and Co., 1901), 5, 331.
13. Both quotations from Frank Norris, *Responsibilities of the Novelist* (New York: Doubleday, Doran, 1928), 21, 167.
14. Irving Kolodin, *The Metropolitan Opera, 1883–1966* (New York: Alfred Knopf, 1966), 133.
15. John H. Mueller, *The American Symphony Orchestra: A Social History of Musical Taste* (Bloomington: Indiana University Press, 1951), 293.
16. Ralph Fletcher Seymour, *Some Went This Way* (Chicago: p.p., 1945), 11.
17. See John Tasker Howard, *Our American Music* (New York: Thomas Crowell, 1965), 323ff; Neil Leonard, 'Edward MacDowell and the Realists', *American Quarterly*, 18 (Summer

1966), 175–82; Hamlin Garland, *Companions on the Trail* (New York: Macmillan, 1932), 376–81.

18. Lawrence Gilman, *Edward MacDowell* (New York: John Lane Co., 1908), 36.

19. Neil Harris, *The Artist in American Society: The Formative Years, 1790–1860* (New York: George Braziller, 1966), 136.

20. William Innes Homer, *Robert Henri and His Circle* (Ithaca: Cornell University Press, 1969), 42.

21. John Rewald, *The History of Impressionism* (New York: Museum of Modern Art, 1946), 21.

22. Quoted in Frank Jewett Mather, Jr, *Modern Painting* (New York: Henry Holt, 1927), 100.

23. Homer, *Robert Henri and His Circle*, 43.

24. Dorothy Weir Young, *The Life and Letters of J. Alden Weir* (New Haven: Yale University Press, 1960), 146.

25. Edwin H. Blashfield, *Mural Painting in America* (New York: Charles Scribner's Sons, 1913), 190. The question of influence is always debatable, and it is easy to find suggestions of some previous artist's work in another painter's output. William Morris Hunt probably had the best reply to a man who suggested that one of his paintings resembled Velasquez: 'Yes, yes, I don't know that I was thinking of Velasquez when it was painted, but possibly if Velasquez had never painted his picture this might not have been done.' Henry C. Angell, *Records of William M. Hunt* (Boston: J. R. Osgood Co., 1880), 13–14.

26. Edgar P. Richardson, *Painting in America* (New York: Thomas Crowell, 1956), 279.

27. Will H. Low, *A Chronicle of Friendships, 1873–1900* (New York: Charles Scribner's Sons, 1908), 232.

28. Frank Jewett Mather, Jr, *Estimates in Art: Second Series* (New York: Henry Holt, 1931), 309.

29. Angell, *Records of William M. Hunt*, 100ff. See Marian Lawrence Peabody, *To Be Young Was Very Heaven* (Boston: Houghton Mifflin Co., 1967), 73ff, for an engaging description of life in art school.

30. See Neil Harris, 'The Gilded Age Revisited: Boston and the Museum Movement', *American Quarterly*, 14 (Winter 1962), 454–66; Lawrence W. Chisolm, *Fenollosa: The Far East and American Culture* (New Haven: Yale University Press, 1963), 123–5.

31. Sadakichi Hartmann, *A History of American Art*, 2 vols. (New York: L. C. Page Co., 1902), II, 284.
32. Theodore Child, *Art and Criticism* (New York: Harper Bros., 1892), 80.
33. Royal Cortissoz, *John La Farge* (Boston: Houghton Mifflin Co., 1911), 107.
34. George W. Sheldon, *Hours With Art and Artists* (New York: D. Appleton Co., 1882), 144–5.
35. Oliver W. Larkin, *Art and Life in America* (New York: Holt, Rinehart and Winston, 1960), 277.
36. Mather, *Estimates in Art*, II, 209.
37. McSpadden, *Famous Painters of America*, 344.
38. Richardson, *Painting in America*, 303.
39. Mather, *Estimates in Art*, II, 307.
40. Quoted in Lorinda Munson Bryant, *American Pictures and Their Painters* (New York: John Lane Co., 1917), 118–19.
41. Hartmann, *History of American Art*, II, 213.
42. Clarence Cook, *Art and Artists of Our Time*, 3 vols. (New York: Selmar Hess, Publisher, 1888), III, 288–9.
43. Peabody, *To Be Young Was Very Heaven*, 295ff.
44. McSpadden, *Famous Painters of America*, 1907.
45. Angell, *Records of William M. Hunt*, 2–3.
46. Dana, *Young in New York*, 147.
47. Knowlton, *W. M. Hunt's Talks on Art*, (First Series), 1, 4.
48. See Rewald, *History of Impressionism*, 394ff; Royal Cortissoz, *Personalities in Art* (New York: Charles Scribner's Sons, 1925).
49. See Barbara Novak, *American Painting of the Nineteenth Century* (New York: Frederick Praeger, 1969), 59, 91, 129–31, 147–8, 169, 243–4.
50. Child, *Art and Criticism*, 162–7.
51. Caffin, *The Story of American Painting*, 269.
52. Mather, *Modern Painting*, 218.
53. Homer, *Robert Henri and His Circle*, 82–3.
54. H. J. Morris, *Confessions in Art* (New York: Sears Pub. Co., 1930), 88; and Harris, *The Artist in American Society*, 295.
55. Both quotations in Young, *Life and Letters of J. Alden Weir*, 178. 188.
56. Allen Tucker, *John H. Twachtman* (New York: Whitney Museum, 1931), 9.
57. Denys Sutton, *Nocturne: The Art of James McNeill Whistler* (Philadelphia: J. B. Lippincott, 1964), 104.

58. ibid., 130.
59. Donald Holden, *Whistler Landscapes and Seascapes* (New York: Watson, Guptil Publishers, 1969), 74.
60. Blashfield, *Mural Painting in America*, 3.
61. Charles Caffin, in Herbert Small [ed.], *Handbook of the New Library of Congress* (Boston: Curtis and Cameron, 1899), 122.
62. Blashfield, *Mural Painting in America*, 27.
63. ibid., 73–4.
64. Pauline King, *American Mural Painting* (Boston: Noyes and Platt, 1902), 146.
65. Fuller, *Under the Skylights*, 172, 260.
66. Hartmann, *History of American Art*, II, 245.

CHAPTER FOUR

A World Role

1. This point is worth remembering. Historians too often create a logical development for foreign policy after reading plans and other materials that were not acted upon. For an engaging and candid statement about the disorder that often accompanies foreign policy planning, see George F. Kennan, *Memoirs, 1925–1950* (New York: Little, Brown Co., 1967), 348–9.
2. Frances Carpenter [ed.], *Carp's Washington* (New York: McGraw-Hill, 1960), 83.
3. Harrison to Whitelaw Reid, 14 December 1891, Whitelaw Reid papers, Library of Congress.
4. Glyndon G. Van Deusen, *William H. Seward* (New York: Oxford University Press, 1967), 532.
5. John A. S. Grenville and George Berkeley Young, *Politics, Strategy and American Diplomacy* (New Haven: Yale University Press, 1966), 10.
6. Walter La Feber, *The New Empire* (Ithaca: Cornell University Press, 1963), 58.
7. Foster Rhea Dulles, *Prelude to World Power* (New York: Macmillan Co., 1965), 124.
8. Chandler to John Sherman, 26 June 1890, John Sherman papers, Library of Congress.
9. Bayard to George H. Pendleton, 9 September 1885, Thomas F. Bayard papers, Library of Congress.
10. Platt to Wharton Barker, 28 January 1885, Wharton Barker

papers, Library of Congress. The Monroe Doctrine did not apply to Cuba, and only opposed the establishment of new European colonies after 1823. But most Americans loosely assumed it expressed the right to oppose European enclaves of whatever origin in the hemisphere.

11. James G. Blaine, *Political Discussions* (Norwich, Conn.: Henry Bill Pub. Co., 1887), 414–15.

12. Quoted in La Feber, *The New Empire*, 71.

13. See Dorothea Muller, 'Josiah Strong and American Nationalism: A Re-evaluation', *Journal of American History*, 53 (December 1966), 487–503; La Feber, *The New Empire*, 16; and A. P. Thornton, *Doctrines of Imperialism* (New York: John Wiley and Sons, 1965), 10, 49, 112.

14. Lodge to S. M. Weld, 19 December 1896, Henry Cabot Lodge papers, Massachusetts Historical Society.

15. Lodge to Henry Higginson, 26 December 1895, ibid.

16. *Papers Relating to the Foreign Relations of the United States, 1897* (Washington: G.P.O., 1898), 540–48; hereafter cited as *For. Rels.*, by date.

17. Accounts that depict McKinley as a businessman's president, primarily representing conservative northeastern interests, are wide of the mark. He was actually a typical midwesterner, heading a diverse political coalition. Ernest R. May, *Imperial Democracy* (New York: Harcourt-Brace, 1961), 112–15, has such an incorrect view. La Feber, *The New Empire*, 284–406, overstates an economic thesis.

18. Quoted in Grenville and Young, *Politics, Strategy and American Diplomacy*, 239–40.

19. Quoted in Charles S. Olcott, *Life of William McKinley*, 2 vols. (Boston: Houghton Mifflin Co., 1916), II, 346.

20. George F. Hoar, *Autobiography of Seventy Years*, 2 vols. (New York: Charles Scribner's Sons, 1903), II, 46.

21. Memorandum dated May 1897, in Box 1, John Bassett Moore papers, Library of Congress.

22. Calhoun's report, dated 22 June 1897, is filed in Special Agents Reports, vol. 48, Record Group 59, National Archives; hereafter cited as RG by number, NA.

23. Grenville and Young, *Politics, Strategy and American Diplomacy*, 247, n.13; *Washington Post*, 25 May 1897.

24. Woodford to Sherman, 16 October 1897, *For. Rels., 1898*, p.

581; Lee to Day, 8 June 1897, Consular Letters from Havana, RG 59 NA.

25. Woodford to McKinley, 24 September 1897, vol. 131A, Dispatches from Spain, RG 59 NA.

26. See Washington *Post*, 6–8 December 1897, for comment on the message and policy. The quote is from W. D. Sloan to Russell Alger, 8 December 1897, Russell Alger papers, William L. Clements Library, Ann Arbor, Michigan.

27. Lodge to Albert Griffin, 31 December 1897, Lodge papers.

28. *Spanish Diplomatic Correspondence and Documents, 1896–1900* (Washington: G.P.O., 1905), 63–7.

29. The letter's text is printed in *For. Rels.*, *1898*, pp. 1007–8; see also, H. Wayne Morgan, 'The De Lome Letter: A New Appraisal', *The Historian*, 26 (November 1963), 36–49; and Grenville and Young, *Politics, Strategy and American Diplomacy*, 253–5.

30. William R. Day feared that history would be too harsh with McKinley, and in 1900 asked the State Department's expert on international law, John Bassett Moore, to write a history of the intervention: '. . . the diplomatic history of that period, to be really intelligible, should be supplemented by an account of the condition of affairs in Cuba, the failure of the proposed reforms, the lack of real self-government in the proposed autonomy [plan], in short the general failure of the Spanish promises and plans for the betterment of conditions in Cuba.' Day to Moore, 24 December 1900, Moore papers, Library of Congress.

31. Hay to Whitelaw Reid, 29 November 1898, John Hay papers, Library of Congress.

32. Robert L. Beisner, *Twelve Against Empire: The Anti-Imperialists, 1898–1900* (New York: McGraw-Hill, 1967), 30.

33. See Christopher Lasch, 'The Anti-Imperialists, The Philippines, and the Equality of Man', *Journal of Southern History*, 24 (August 1958), 310–31.

34. *Congressional Record*, 55th Congress, 2nd Session, 5790–92.

Index